Why Don't We Say **What We Mean?**

Why Don't We Say **What We Mean?**

ESSAYS MOSTLY ABOUT POETRY

Lawrence Raab

T|P

TUPELO PRESS
North Adams, Massachusetts

Why Don't We Say What We Mean?
Copyright © 2016 Lawrence Raab. All rights reserved.

Library of Congress Cataloging-in-Publication Data
Names: Raab, Lawrence, 1946- author.
Title: Why don't we say what we mean? : essays mostly about poetry /
    Lawrence Raab.
Other titles: Tupelo Press's Life in art series.
Description: North Adams, Massachusetts : Tupelo Press, [2016] | Series:
    Tupelo Press's Life in art series
Identifiers: LCCN 2016050126 | ISBN 9781936797769 (pbk. original : alk.
paper)
Subjects: LCSH: Poetry. | Poetry--History and criticism.
Classification: LCC PN1031 .R23 2016 | DDC 808.1—dc23

Cover and text designed by Howard Klein.
Cover painting: "Cadmium Orange of Dr. Frankenstein" (1962), by Jules
Olitski. Acrylic on canvas, 90 ³/₈ x 80 in. Copyright © Estate of Jules Olitski,
licensed by VAGA, New York, NY. Gift from the Vincent Melzac Collection,
Smithsonian Art Museum. Photo credit: Smithsonian Art Museum,
Washington, DC / Art Resource, NY. Used with permission.

First paperback edition: December 2016.

Tupelo Press
P.O. Box 1767, North Adams, Massachusetts 01247
(413) 664-9611 / editor@tupelopress.org / www.tupelopress.org

ART WORKS.
arts.gov

Supported in part by an award from the National Endowment for the Arts.

for Charles Scott and John Plant

People say, "Why don't you say what you mean?"
We never do that, do we, being all of us too much poets.

—*Robert Frost, from his essay "Education by Poetry: A Meditative Monologue" (1931)*

Contents

1

Not Knowing

"It is true," Emily Dickinson wrote, "that the unknown is the largest need of the intellect, though for it, no one thinks to thank God." Following her lead, we might also wish to thank God for his unwillingness to reveal himself, for all that is hidden, and for the value, finally, of not knowing. And then we should be grateful as well for those works of art that appear to present their true and authentic selves only to undermine our confidence upon a closer reading, and so make larger and more surprising demands on our imaginations.

In his essay "Lost off Cape Wrath," the novelist and critic John Berger maintains that authenticity in literature comes from "a single faithfulness"—to the ambiguity of experience, not the writer's personal honesty—and he argues that unless a writer is driven by a desire for the most demanding verbal precision, "the true ambiguity of events escapes him." But one strategy of a poem can be to conceal the complications of experience behind an unde-manding screen of simplicity—behind, that is, a seemingly sincere and unambiguous way of perceiving the world.

A master of this unsettling tactic is Edwin Arlington Robinson. Consider his most famous poem:

Richard Cory

Whenever Richard Cory went down town,
We people on the pavement looked at him:
He was a gentleman from sole to crown,
Clean favored, and imperially slim.

And he was always quietly arrayed,
And he was always human when he talked;
But still he fluttered pulses when he said,
"Good morning," and he glittered when he walked.

And he was rich—yes, richer than a king—
And admirably schooled in every grace:
In fine, we thought that he was everything
to make us wish that we were in his place.

So on we worked, and waited for the light,
And went without the meat, and cursed the bread;
And Richard Cory, one calm summer night,
Went home and put a bullet through his head.

Many critics have dismissed that ending as an all-too-obvious trick. But whose trick is it—Robinson's, or his speaker's? It seems to me that if you accept the ending as no more than a calculated surprise, then you yourself have been deceived by the poem just as the townspeople have deceived themselves about the character of Richard Cory. They choose to see him as glittering and imperial, "richer than a king," god-like, totally apart and excluded from the human community they represent. They do not question their perception of him. They do not suppose that their response to him—a kind of awestruck shunning of the different—could have any connection to his suicide. They have their self-pitying yet self-congratulatory logic, and the reader can easily be lured into becoming one of them. The trick of the ending is directed as much toward the unwary reader as it is reflective of the unperceptive character of the townspeople who narrate the poem. Cory is typecast and his death turned into a cliché—Money can't buy happiness. The speakers of "Richard Cory" have reduced the unknown to an effective story with a snappy ending. I imagine them being proud of this. But the precision of Robinson's language contains what has escaped them: the mystery of human action and experience. Not knowing. But knowing that we do not know.

Ambiguity, we might say, is an awareness of complexity that leads to uncertainty, to that state of remaining in doubt about what we wish to understand. Thomas Hardy's "The Shadow on the Stone" beautifully enacts the complications of this problem:

The Shadow on the Stone

> I went by the Druid stone
> That broods in the garden white and lone,
> And I stopped and looked at the shifting shadows
> That at some moments fall thereon
> From the tree hard by with a rhythmic swing,
> And they shaped in my imagining
> To the shade that a well-known head and shoulders
> Threw there when she was gardening.
>
> I thought her behind my back,
> Yea, her I long had learned to lack,
> And I said: 'I am sure you are standing behind me,
> Though how do you get into this old track?'
> And there was no sound but the fall of a leaf
> As a sad response; and to keep down my grief

I would not turn my head to discover
    That there was nothing in my belief.

    Yet I wanted to look and see
    That nobody stood at the back of me;
  But I thought once more: 'Nay, I'll not unvision
    A shape which, somehow, there may be.'
    So I went on softly from the glade,
    And left her behind me throwing her shade,
  As she were indeed an apparition—
    My head unturned lest my dream should fade.

Hardy cannot escape—indeed he employs—a kind of radical ambiguity in this poem. His imagination shapes those "shifting shadows" into an image of his dead wife ("her I long had learned to lack"), and then grants that imagining so much reality that he speaks to her: "'I am sure you are standing behind me . . .'" Then reality becomes "my belief," which he refuses to deny by turning his head to discover what he knows to be true—that no woman has been formed from those all-too-ordinary shadows.

Still, he wants to look; he wants to see the nothing that he knows is there, while at the same moment he wants the opposite: not to "unvision /A shape which, somehow, there may be." To "unvision" that shape would be to dispel all of the ambiguity of the moment, but he refuses. That *shape*—no longer "her"—may be there. That "somehow" suggests a force beyond his understanding. Yet the poem also refuses to identify such a force. Is it religious? Is it pagan?—that "Druid stone" so carefully placed in the first sentence that we can easily forget its momentarily personified presence? It "broods," as does the poet. Or is it Hardy's shaping imagination that places him at the edge of understanding, and of deception?

Hardy will not choose. Or else he chooses to remain in a state of uncertainty—of what *may* be, though he truly knows it *cannot* be. The essential turn of the poem is the "Yet" that begins the final stanza, followed by the surprise that he *wants* to look back to see that nothing is there. He wishes to be disillusioned. But he wishes to remain in doubt.

The poem's most striking word is "unvision," which would be the act of destroying an imaginative creation—her presence—which he understands is an illusion, and wishes to prove an illusion, *and yet* wishes most of all to leave alone, allowing the possibility of mystery to remain. (". . . reciprocal ambiguities coalesce into a mystery," John Berger writes.) Hardy walks away and she is left "behind me throwing her shade," as if for a moment she were not the ghostly "shade" itself, but the real person casting her shadow. But the poem allows for one more disturbing "as if" in its penultimate line: "As she were indeed an apparition . . ." Indeed—in truth—she might be *only* an apparition, but the poem has proven much less: that she is neither a shade nor a person who could cast a shade, but simply "my dream." In this poem Hardy raises ambiguity to the highest, most authentic imaginative level.

But what does authenticity—a concept Berger links to ambiguity—mean in a poem? Let's say a poem is authentic when the poet transforms the personal into a structure that supports what *the poem* itself wants us to believe. "To tell the truth," T. S. Eliot writes, "is a technical achievement." This suggests that the writer's own sincerity or insincerity remains essentially irrelevant to the effect of the poem. Indeed, the available truth of the poem may not even be the truth that was intended.

Fernando Pessoa speaks of "a translated sincerity" that, he claims, "is the basis of all art." The feelings of the writer are translated through the artifice of the poem into the feelings of the poem, into a verbal precision that transcends the writer's personal honesty. But of course that doesn't mean that the *speaker* of the poem is to be trusted. Think again of "Richard Cory":

> And he was always quietly arrayed,
> And he was always human when he talked . . .

So much is betrayed by the speaker's assertion that Cory was "always human"—in some way like them but in most ways not. However modest—however *human*—he strives to be, Cory will always appear "arrayed." Discovering the truth of the poem behind the assumptions of the speaker is the reader's task.

Therefore, in Pessoa's terms there may be two kinds of translation taking place. The first is the poet's translation of his or her own thoughts—however conflicted or uncertain—into an appropriate level of complication (in "Richard Cory" the complications of the word "human"). The second involves the reader's translation of the speaker's assertions into a structure that discloses the truth of the poem (what that use of the word "human" reveals about "we people on the pavement," and then about humanity in general).

To quote Berger once more: "It is the writer's openness to the ambiguity and uncertainty of any experience (even the expression of determination and certainty) which gives clarity, and thus a kind of certitude to his writing." Note that this certitude is in the writing, not the life. And note that what is produced is a *kind* of certitude, which may be a *kind* of ambiguity.

Now consider another poem by Thomas Hardy:

The Oxen

Christmas Eve, and twelve of the clock.
　　"Now they are all on their knees,"
An elder said as we sat in a flock
　　By the embers in hearthside ease.

We pictured the meek mild creatures where
　　They dwelt in their strawy pen,
Nor did it occur to one of us there
　　To doubt they were kneeling then.

So fair a fancy few would weave
　　In these years! Yet, I feel,
If someone said on Christmas Eve,
　　"Come; see the oxen kneel,

"In the lonely barton by yonder coomb
　　Our childhood used to know,"
I should go with him in the gloom,
　　Hoping it might be so.

This poem is balanced between the unexamined certitude of childhood and the disbelief of the present. The apparent truth of religious revelation has become only a fireside tale, yet it is still a story of compelling power, since behind it (for some) lies a larger belief that might at least offer ease, or comfort, in "these times." (The poem was first published on Christmas Eve of 1915.)

Hardy is not anxious to prove that an old Christmas tale must be a fiction. The story, after all, belongs to the innocent past, that "lonely barton by yonder comb / Our childhood used to know." But in the poem he says that, if asked, he would go to see those oxen kneel. Yet he does not go. The poem requires only that he *feel* he might. As a child among children, listening to an elder, it did not "occur to one of us / To doubt . . . " Now he would have to see to believe. And so he will not "unvision" what is not there.

Authenticity may be the writer's most important aim, but the unknown still remains the mind's largest need.

Should Poems Tell the Truth?

Midway through my freshman year at college, my room-mate Roger asked if I would read a poem he'd written and tell him what I thought. I was pleased to be considered a literary person whose opinion might be valued. And my roommate, who would major in geology, had previously shown no interest in poetry. "Of course," I said.

The subject of the poem was the death of Roger's father, and reading it I felt a small shock, since no one I knew had yet lost a parent. Unfortunately, Roger's poem was very bad. I don't remember now the various ways in which it failed, but there seemed no doubt in my mind. Given the subject, however, what kind of criticism would be appropriate or bearable?

I began by expressing my condolences, and Roger interrupted quickly to say, No, his father hadn't really died. That was just the subject of the poem. "But you can't do that!" I exclaimed. Perhaps I didn't actually exclaim, or even say it directly. But it was what I felt. This was wrong, a violation of some rule or code. You couldn't do it, or you shouldn't.

But why not? What if the poem had been good? Would I have condemned it because it wasn't "true"? Would factual truth have been transformed into a larger "truth" (quotation marks intended), as determined by literary value?

Roger's poem was called "On the Death of My Father," a title that laid the subject out and announced the identity of the speaker. I entered the poem with certain information, but also a series of assumptions about the truth. A somewhat similar—but finally very different— example to consider is this sonnet by Weldon Kees:

For My Daughter

Looking into my daughter's eyes I read
Beneath the innocence of morning flesh
Concealed, hintings of death she does not heed.
Coldest of winds have blown this hair, and mesh
Of seaweed snarled these miniatures of hands;
The night's slow poison, tolerant and bland,
Has moved her blood. Parched years that I have seen
That may be hers appear: foul, lingering
Death in certain war, the slim legs green.
Or, fed on hate, she relishes the sting
Of others' agony; perhaps the cruel
Bride of a syphilitic or a fool.
These speculations sour in the sun.
I have no daughter. I desire none.

The shock of the last line depends upon the reader's assumption that the poet has a daughter; that the title, in other words, tells the truth. A more accurate title, like "Unpleasant Speculations About Fatherhood," wouldn't sufficiently prepare for the twist at the end. (How effective this move remains on repeated readings is a separate problem.) But there's no doubt that the final two sentences, on a first reading, are a significant surprise, and that the surprise depends upon an assumption about factual truth. I suspect that even readers who are theoretically disposed to keeping truth inside a set of quotation marks, who believe all "truths" are inventions, would be taken in by Kees's poem. The title is, after all, so conventional it doesn't seem to be hiding anything. However wary we have become, no one starts reading a poem entitled "For My Wife" by immediately wondering if the poet really has a wife. We can't be suspicious of everything.

We feel manipulated by Kees but not betrayed. If the poem is at all successful, the bleakness of its conclusion also produces a kind of literary pleasure, the reward of the sprung trap. And in this way the subject of the poem enlarges to include, beyond the poet's despairing sense of life, the nature of readerly expectation and response. Poems that correct themselves within themselves, as Kees's poem does at the last minute, stake out a territory in which claims about the truth are important. At about the same time I found the Kees poem I came upon Donald Finkel's "Target Practice," which begins:

> On the first day good enough father and son
> Went out with the new gun
> And rode for miles in Iowa.
>
> No. That spring, city-bred and new to sun,
> We went out in the car in Iowa
> And parked at last between
> Two farms and walked, through mud, to the place.

> Neither is right, the fiction
> Or the fact. It is as if
> What happened were good enough . . .

Finkel's "No" was a revelation for me. The poem wasn't just *about* how fiction tries to improve on fact, or how memory is fiction; it was a dramatization of those concerns. The first stanza invites belief, just as Kees's title did—a story, third-person narrative, set in a real place, Iowa. Then what it gave it takes away: *No.* Think again. Try it a different way. After this move, the speculation ("Neither is right . . . ") feels somewhat disappointing, as if the poem were saying: Well, we've had our metaphysical fun, now let's figure this out. Finkel does manage to complicate things, but it's the beginning of the poem that still arrests me: the excitement of fact giving way to fiction, of the imagined trying to do the work of the merely true.

Inept as Roger's poem about his father was, its major disappointment was that it hadn't tried to use the lie it gave itself. The elegy for the father who isn't dead is a compelling premise. But the literal truth has to be replaced by an emotional truth. Perhaps the father is in all ways dead to the son except that he hasn't actually died. The poem needs to find a way to acknowledge this, not because it's an obligation to set the record straight, but because the poem doesn't *work* without finding some way to expand the lie to involve the reader. Still, what if it hadn't chosen that route and had just been written better? If I had read "On the Death of My Father" in a magazine, and I knew nothing about the poet, and I was moved, and never learned it was all an invention, would I have been *wrong* to be moved? If I learned the facts, how would I feel?

I don't remember when I first read Robert Lowell's *Paris Review* interview, and discovered that "Skunk Hour" wasn't altogether true, that the incident of voyeurism in the graveyard was "not mine, but borrowed from an anecdote about Walt Whitman in his old age." When I read Lowell's interview I was preparing to teach the poem in the context of "confessionalism," and I was aware that many of these poets were angry at being defined in this way. (When asked in *his* interview in the *Paris Review* how he reacted to the label of "confessional poet," John Berryman replied, "With rage and contempt! Next question.")

The Walt Whitman anecdote generates useful questions for a teacher. I knew Lowell suffered from manic breakdowns, so the essence of the poem was real, and his own. Was it somehow permissible to invent small facts but not large ones? The success of the poem, and its fame, and its important position as the "anchor poem" (as Lowell calls it) in an immensely influential book, *Life Studies*, all combine to complicate the issue. Lowell himself complicates it further in the interview:

> They're not always factually true. There's a good deal of tinkering with fact. You leave out a lot, and emphasize this and not that. Your actual experience is a complete flux. I've invented facts and changed things, and the whole balance of the poem was something invented. So there's a lot of artistry, I hope, in the poems. Yet there's this thing: if a poem is autobiographical—and this is true of any kind of autobiographical writing and of historical

writing—you want the reader to say, this is true. In something like Macaulay's *History of England* you think you're really getting William III. That's as good as a good plot in a novel. And so there was always that standard of truth which you wouldn't have in poetry—the reader was to believe he was getting the *real* Robert Lowell.

The "standard of truth" Lowell chooses for himself is not fidelity to biographical fact, but the *appearance* of fidelity. Lowell's brief segue into the second person—"You leave out a lot, and emphasize this or that"—suggests an awareness that he knows he's speaking in part for poets in general. Therefore the representation of the self in a poem is always a kind of fiction. The life is long and messy, the poem short and revisable. The "whole balance" of every poem is always an invention. Lowell's particular project in *Life Studies* makes the additional demand that the reader be unaware of this "tinkering with fact." *Life Studies* claims the authority of history: "the reader was to believe he was getting the *real* Robert Lowell."

Lowell states that in "any kind" of autobiographical and historical writing "you want the reader to say, this is true." The writer who presents his work as fiction, however much it makes use of the autobiographical, tells the reader to pay attention to the work itself. The *transformation* of the personal is what's important. By making the opposite assertion—conflating speaker and poet to present "the real," Lowell risks that personal confession will overwhelm artistry, not in the making of the poem, but for some readers.

For example, the poet Phillip Booth, who owned a house in Maine and knew Lowell, tells a story of meeting in a laundromat in Castine "a vacationing schoolteacher from Bangor, a woman I grew up with." "You write poetry sometimes, don't you?" the woman says, and Booth admits he does. "Will you tell me," the woman continues, "*how* a poet like Mr. Lowell can be so famous when he can't even get Jimmy Sawyer on the right island? . . . Everybody knows that that woman on Nautilus [in "Skunk Hour"] never had children, and that Jimmy Sawyer keeps the farm for Miss Harris over on *Hol*brook Island!"

How could a "famous" poet get the facts so wrong? And how can we believe anything he has to say if he can't get his islands straight? The factual truth here is the bottom line.

Whereas the fictive immediately calls attention to form, the autobiographical is essentially shapeless. There's always more of it. Biographical detail—mere anecdote and gossip—can overwhelm the assertion of form, and form is at the heart of *Life Studies.*

In *Life Studies* the book, "Life Studies" the sequence is preceded by a prose memoir, "91 Revere Street," which should be read as an essential part of both book and sequence. "91 Revere Street" (now too often separated from its book and included in Lowell's prose) seems to provide background material, and it does. It's lively, entertaining, and poignant in and of itself. But in context it asserts itself as a "standard of truth," the believability of prose.

On the whole, Lowell said in the interview, "prose is less cut off from life than poetry is." Whether or not this is true is less important than the fact that it seems to be true. Prose is diffuse, like life; poetry is a fine distillation. While Lowell's prose is wonderfully controlled, "91 Revere Street" is designed to appear both diffuse and incomplete. It doesn't move in a straight line but circles around, as if trying to describe or define or even uncover its real subject. Its amiability and pacing put the reader off guard, attentive to details and anecdotes for their own sakes, lulled by the pleasures of good storytelling. Readers may complain that the prose holds up the book. It does, and is intended to.

The book's final section escapes from "91 Revere Street." The movement from prose back into poetry emphasizes the properties of a poem as a poem. The "truth" of experience (that is, of prose) is set in a tension with the artifice of poetry. But both are concerned with the issue—indeed the drama—of form. While working on these poems, Lowell says he came to "have a certain disrespect for the tight forms." Regularity "just seemed to ruin the honesty of sentiment, and became rhetorical; it said, 'I'm a poem.'"

However, Lowell doesn't choose to abandon form as much as disguise it. The prosiness of free verse is set against the partially deconstructed architecture of rhyme and meter. In "Commander Lowell," for example, Lowell speaks of the usefulness of "the original skeleton" of four-foot couplets. "I could keep the couplets where I wanted them and drop them when I didn't; there'd be a form to come back to." The ghosts of form in the "Life Studies" sequence are linked to the apparent lack of form in the prose of "91 Revere Street," making the book as a whole about attempts to find form—and therefore meaning—within a life, or to impose it on a life.

The structures of privilege displayed in "91 Revere Street" are falling apart, though the young Lowell can't see it happening. The mother clings to what the father cannot support, what the house and the history of the family cannot support, and what is passed on from parents to child is the desire for a structure, even one that is disintegrating. In "91 Revere Street," appropriately named for the place that contains the family, the process leads to Commander Harkness's crude remark at the end: "I know why young Bob is an only child." After the brief, ominous pause of Part Three—four elegiac poems about writers—the apparent calm and comfort of anecdotal prose releases Part Four—the "Life Studies" poems—in a fury of incident, so that the individual, the poet, the real Robert Lowell we have been asked to believe in, is all but overwhelmed. The death of Uncle Devereux Winslow is followed by the death of the grandparents, then of the father, then the mother, which is followed by (or leads to) Lowell's own madness and hospitalization, the birth of his daughter, the tensions in his marriage, and finally "Skunk Hour."

Earlier I asked a question I didn't answer: If I had read my roommate's elegy for his father in a magazine (assuming that it was a much better poem), and I was moved, and then later learned it was all an invention, would I feel betrayal or admiration? I'm still not sure how I would answer, and perhaps that's because I've set up too simple a situation.

If I admired the poem before, why should the literal truth cause a change of mind? Shouldn't I continue to admire it as a poem? But how would I feel if, after many readings of *Life Studies*, I learned that Lowell had had a wonderfully happy childhood, never suffered from manic breakdowns, had always made his home in Iowa, and never even visited Boston or Maine? Two responses spring to mind:

(1) What an imagination that guy has!
(2) What a fraud that guy is!

Both seem inevitable, while neither feels adequate. I could imagine thinking, *I wish I hadn't known that*, the way we feel when we discover a favorite writer was a member of the Nazi party. But isn't disappointment in the person different from concerns about art? Why should the art change? Two responses again occur to me:

(1) Because the art *does* change, unless we can wholly separate it from its creator.
(2) Because the allure of this particular piece of art—*Life Studies*—was the promise of the personal, since we were carefully led to believe we were getting "the *real* Robert Lowell."

The personal, of course, was not the end, but the means. Self-revelation is a strategy. Therefore, should discovering that we weren't getting the real Robert Lowell change anything? Should poems tell the truth? The easy answer to that question is: Yes, but the truth of poetry is different from the truth of life. Then the interesting complications lie in the word "different."

An early draft of "Skunk Hour" titled "Inspiration" ends with a single skunk:

My headlights glare
On a galvanized bucket crumpling up—
A skunk glares in a garbage pail.
It jabs its trowel-head in a cup
Of sour cream, drops its ostrich tail,
And cannot scare.

The final version has a family of skunks:

I stand on top
of our back steps and breathe the rich air—
a mother skunk with her column of kittens swills
    the garbage pail.
She jabs her wedge-head in a cup
of sour cream, drops her ostrich tail,
and will not scare.

No one would be troubled if it were shown that
Lowell actually saw only one skunk, or that he saw a
raccoon and changed it to a family of skunks for the sake
of the poem. Few would be upset if it were discovered
that Lowell made the whole ending up, or that it was yet
another anecdote ascribed to Walt Whitman in his old age.
In the poem Lowell declares, "My mind's not right." And
I've suggested that we might justifiably feel concerned
should it be revealed that Lowell's mind was always right
and his life untroubled. But this leads to the worrisome
proposition that big things count but small ones don't.
And that may be true. But it also doesn't feel adequate.
Let's avoid the matter for the moment by returning to
Weldon Kees, whose poem asks us to maneuver among

different kinds of truths, finally acknowledging itself as literally made-up. In this way the stakes of the poem are changed. The apparent subject—the horrors Kees imagines for his daughter—gives way to the act of invention, and the reader's complicity in that act.

This leads back to one assertion, if not exactly one conclusion: that a successful poem must in some way acknowledge the reader. As Paul Valéry writes in "Poetry and Abstract Thought": "A poet's function—do not be startled by this remark—is not to experience the poetic state: that is a private affair. His function is to create it in others." Yet young writers *are* often startled by that remark. The poem is made for the reader, and is sent out into the world to do its work as best it can, and without any intervention from the author. As Richard Wilbur has said, the poem is "a kind of machine of feeling which other people can use." The rest is private.

So the truth of a poem is the *poem's* truth. But if it uses facts from the poet's life, it needs to manage those facts for the reader. That still does not answer the question of Big Invention vs. Small Invention, a reconstituted life vs. an extra skunk or two. But I think figuring the reader into the equation may give us a way of approaching these complications.

In an interview in 1916 for the *Philadelphia Public Ledger*, Robert Frost is quoted as saying, "Never larrup an emotion. Set yourself against the moon. Resist the moon. If the moon's going to do anything to you, it's up to the moon." Frost ends the interview by becoming even more provocative. "The curse of our poetry," he says, "is that we lay it on things. Pocketsful of poetic adjectives like pocketsful of peanuts carried into a park for the gray squirrels! You can take it as gospel, that's not what we want. But people say to me: 'The facts aren't enough. You've got to do something to them, haven't you? They can't be poetical unless a poet handles them.' To that I have a very simple answer. It's this: 'Anything you do to the facts falsifies them, but anything the facts do to you—yes, even against your will; yes, resist them with all your strength—transforms them into poetry.'"

How exactly can we think about this claim concerning the action of facts? First of all, I don't find this to be "a very simple answer." Nor is the question simple, which I believe Frost knew. It all seems to me a setup, passing off sophisticated thinking as mere "Yankee wisdom." I find it impossible to imagine any person—not to mention more than one—actually saying to Frost, "The facts aren't enough. You've got to do something to them ... " And so on. We're tricked into agreement without really knowing what we've agreed to.

Another sort of trick here is Frost's move from "poetical" to "poetry." The writer who merely "handles" the facts can only enhance them into the "poetical," a kind of false, pretentious language that ends up being at best comfortable and pretty rather than challenging and beautiful. This is the writer with his pockets full of adjectives to lay on the things of the world like a glittery veneer. The revelation Frost calls for requires struggle. Truth (with a capital "T") does not precede the making of the poem but is discovered in it through resistance to those truths that are too easy and predictable.

Poets, therefore, must set themselves "against the

moon." To simply "larrup" the moon would be to settle for an emotional cliché. Let the moon do some of the work, Frost insists. "It's up to the moon." But more exactly, it's up to the poet's resistance to all of the beguiling moon-moments that can so easily insinuate themselves into a poem. And yet there's still the moon—alluring, compelling, mysterious. Show me, says the wise poet. Show me what you've got.

"Anything you do to the facts falsifies them." But does this first half of Frost's assertion in fact make sense? By itself, I don't think it does, given the vagueness of the word "do." The key seems to be in the reversal: ". . . anything the facts do to you . . . transforms them into poetry." Out of this engagement, in which the truth of the life becomes *material*, the truth of the poem emerges; that is, the discovery of the truth *inside* the fact transforms incident into art.

Presented this way, the issue of the "truth" becomes a matter of artistic strategy: how best to negotiate with the reader, whose relation to the poem is similar to the poet's relation to his material. ("No surprise for the writer," Frost says, "no surprise for the reader.") On the other hand, the poet's negotiations with himself are no less important, though much less apparent to us, unless they are revealed through letters, essays, or interviews. The less we know about the life, the more pressure is put on the machinery of the poem.

Therefore, if Roger's elegy had been a good poem, I would have had to admire it. If then I found out that the father had not died, I hope I would have first re-read the poem to see if that fact existed as part of a deliberate move the poem had, at first, concealed from me, as in the first thirteen lines of Kees's sonnet. But if I found no evidence of that, I would have little reason to feel troubled, though I would probably wonder about the author. What, I now ask myself, would I wonder?

I would wonder if this poem was typical of the author's work. If all of the writing (assuming a more practiced and prolific poet than Roger) displayed similar uses—or distortions—of the literal truth, that would provide a larger context in which to consider the various relations between poet, poem, and reader. If the poet had chosen to be a fiction-maker of a certain kind, I would hope to respect that choice as long as the poems by themselves earned my respect.

I would also wonder—given a substantial body of work—if the poet had created a persona *outside* of the poems. (And here we should acknowledge Fernando Pessoa, who invented more than seventy imaginary writers to stand behind his poems, figures he called "heteronyms" rather than pseudonyms because each possessed a distinct autobiography and a different style. Pessoa's three major figures are Alberto Caeiro, Ricardo Reis, and Álvaro de Campos, and of these Pessoa writes, "Caeiro writes bad Portuguese, Campos writes it reasonably well but with mistakes . . . and Reis writes better than I, but with a purisim I find excessive . . . ") The fictional persona I am wondering about for Roger (whose father is dead) would certainly be less elaborate than Pessoa's creations, but the imaginary life could still slide into, or overshadow, or intentionally disguise, the writer's actual life.

Finally, I would wonder if knowledge of any kind of

manipulation would enhance the work. If the poems were good, could they be better by revealing the ways their materials had been handled? This question suggests an intensification, and complication, of the relation between poem and reader. "Anything the facts do" to the poet can be withheld, or it can be displayed within the poem. So the issue becomes less whether Roger was right or wrong to write what he did, than whether he could have made a better poem by consciously using the possibilities of his invention, by allowing his relationship with truth and falsehood to become part of his thinking as a writer, and then part of the design of his poem.

(It seems important to know that Pessoa created Caeiro, Reis, and Campos, that he stands behind them all, that as separate as they may seem, finally they relate to each other, and are part of a singular endeavor.)

At some point in the act of composition, Robert Lowell must have thought it would be useful to try the "truth" of more than one skunk. Then I imagine he felt what a fine discovery that was—the way the mother and her kittens enlarge the moment, creating a family for the previous lost and desperate man who now watches them from "on top / of *our* back steps" (emphasis mine), and who breathes an air that has become "rich" with the possibilities of survival. In terms of the facts, it's a small change; in terms of an invention pressed upon the poet by his *handling* of the facts, it's enormously effective, and not just as an individual detail, but as a way of representing the most moving and consequential emotions of the poem.

In his remark about prose being "less cut off from life

than poetry," Lowell certainly intends a critique of the constraints of his earlier, highly formal work. To allow the factuality of prose into his poems urged them closer to life and colloquial language. But it's useful to think that there's a value in poetry being *more* "cut off from life" if the distance between the life and the poem allows the poet to make a more effective work of art. It's within this space that Frost's struggle with the facts creates the necessary moment of transformation. What the reader finally encounters is the poem's staged reenactment of what the poet, through resistance, once discovered.

Choosing the Wrong Subject

That poets are praised and blamed for their subject matter is understandable. It's easier to talk about subjects than about poems. And for many it may be hard to distinguish between the two.

A subject, let's say, is what a poem is about, its paraphrasable content. Or as the *Oxford English Dictionary* puts it more elaborately, "that which forms or is chosen as the matter of thought, consideration, or inquiry; a topic, theme." If a subject defines what a poem is about, what a poem *means* is determined by attitude, the "mode of regarding the object of thought," though the *OED* reminds us that attitude's original reference was to the fine arts: "The 'disposition' of a figure in statuary or painting; hence, the posture given to it." Attitude is how the subject is presented, how in a poem the voice postures—therefore tone. Subjects may be prose, but the poet's attitudes lead, line by line, toward the condition of poetry.

To contrast subject and attitude may seem unnecessary. Aren't they sufficiently distinct? Yet I believe that much bad writing—criticism as well as poetry—arises from a confusion of "the matter of thought" and the way thought postures and displays itself.

At the risk of clouding an argument I haven't yet made, one additional distinction may be useful—between subjects and materials. "Matter of thought" would seem to cover both. But when we think of subject as theme, we think of a statement—the transience of the physical world, the inevitability of death. Themes are inevitably reductive. How easy it is to move from the seemingly profound to the obviously ridiculous, as in this wicked *Harvard Lampoon* parody of a college course description: "*English 300: Major Themes That Can't Miss.* Themes so all-encompassing that they cannot possibly be unrelated to any given work of fiction. Motifs to be dealt with include appearance vs. reality, alienation and discovery, good vs. evil, nature vs. art, and the journey."

If themes are reductive, materials are expansive and messy. They are the stuff of a poem—things, images, whatever makes the abstract visible and felt: a bare tree, for example, with a single leaf. Such an image has no inherent meaning or value. Badly handled, it becomes silly: "Grown old, I feel as lonely as a leaf / Atremble in the bitter winds of age." But the same essential material can, of course, be transformed into great art:

> That time of year thou mayst in me behold
> When yellow leaves or none, or few, do hang
> Upon those boughs which shake against the cold,
> Bare ruin'd choirs, where late the sweet birds sang.

Neither Shakespeare's enduring theme, mortality, nor the image, a few leaves on a bare tree, can guarantee a successful poem.

The distinctions I mean to pursue have practical consequences as well. Aren't subjects where we start? Sometimes. But to believe this without question may result in the most common error inexperienced poets are likely to make: to think that one's first sense of a subject should determine the shape and ambitions of the unwritten poem. And "subjects" here can apply either to theme (the inevitability of death), or to a defined set of materials (trees, leaves, wind). Rather than preceding the poem, the subject may more usefully be imagined as declaring itself toward the end of the process of composition, its consequence and discovery. This means that we often only think we know what a poem is about when we start. Or we don't know at all.

Attitude arises from the poet's engagement with a subject. As attitude develops (along with the particular shifts of tone and syntax that enclose and reveal it), the subject expands, or contracts, or changes. If the original subject seemingly disappears, it may not have been displaced so much as deepened. And if it has truly vanished, the poet can return to it later. Another potential poem has presented itself. Maybe better, maybe worse. But there it is, asking for attention. As Robert Frost says of writing in general, "To learn to write is to learn to have ideas." To learn to write a poem is to learn how to have those ideas necessary for that particular poem. In this sense, the making of each poem is an education.

I want now to consider two poems by the same author on similar subjects. Both are elegies in couplets, each twelve lines long; both are by Ben Jonson—one for his daughter, one for his son.

On My First Daughter

Here lies, to each her parents' ruth,
Mary, the daughter of their youth;
Yet all heaven's gifts being heaven's due,

It makes the father less to rue.
At six months' end she parted hence
With safety of her innocence;
Whose soul heaven's queen, whose name she bears,
In comfort of her mother's tears,
Hath placed amongst her virgin-train:
Where, while that severed doth remain,
This grave partakes the fleshly birth;
Which cover lightly, gentle earth.

On My First Son

Farewell, thou child of my right hand, and joy;
My sin was too much hope of thee, lov'd boy.
Seven years tho'wert lent to me, and I thee pay,
Exacted by thy fate, on the just day.
O, could I lose all father now! For why
Will man lament the state he should envy,
To have so soon 'scap'd world's and flesh's rage,
And if no other misery, yet age?
Rest in soft peace, and, ask'd, say, "Here doth lie
Ben Jonson his best piece of poetry."
For whose sake henceforth all his vows be such,
As what he loves may never like too much.

Frequently, I give the following assignment to my students: Which is the better poem, and why? I insist (but am rarely believed) that the assignment is not a trick. Respectable arguments can be made for both. Nor is the point to decide that one of the poems is simply bad. They may be different in ways that do not translate into similar value judgments. In fact, the essential point of the assignment is to struggle with the difficulty of explaining and defending value judgments. Many would argue against the proposition itself. Is it worth making such judgments? Is it even possible? Yes, I want to say. Partly because it's natural for us to have preferences, and therefore important to discover the bases, however personal, of such preferences. Partly because the practicing poet is always in the position of striking one word out in favor of another, thinking, *That's good; that's not so good.* Or: *That works; that doesn't.*

Although I've read good papers arguing for "On My First Daughter," most students quickly side with "On My First Son." The essence of the students' position is this: "Son" is a more emotional poem, therefore better. Jonson, they argue, clearly was closer to his son, who lived for seven years, than to his daughter, who survived a mere six months. Because the son's death was more wrenching, it produced the greater poem. This argument posits a direct relationship between life and art: More powerful experience produces more substantial art. Subject determines value. I want to resist the equation.

Students will often criticize "Daughter" in the following ways: The tetrameter sounds jingly, like a tombstone epitaph, whereas the pentameter of "Son" allows for a more clearly spoken voice. In "Daughter," Jonson speaks of himself in the third person and combines his feelings with those of his wife; thus "Son" is more direct and highly charged, "Daughter" more distanced and impersonal. Finally, in "Daughter" the standard arguments for comfort are asserted and accepted, whereas in "Son" they provoke questions and dispute. All of this seems to me to be true. And yet—isn't it possible to imagine a very good poem in tetrameter that adopts a distant, impersonal voice and chooses not to challenge a set of accepted religious beliefs?

And surely we can imagine a genuinely grief-stricken poet producing a mediocre and unconvincing poem. It must happen all the time. We are not moved by the fact that Jonson's son died. We are moved by the way he handles that death in his poem. If, finally, we feel that "On My First Son" is a better poem than "On My First Daughter," it's not because life provided a better subject, but because that subject led the poet to develop a more compelling set of attitudes. In turn, those attitudes led Jonson to the particular language that distinguishes his poem.

The most striking feature of "Son" is the way it invokes poetry by using its own presence. The dead child, as if being put to bed, is told to "Rest in soft peace." But that peace is immediately interrupted: "and asked, say . . . " The boy, about to sleep, is granted speech, then given a specific sentence: "'Here doth lie / Ben Jonson his best piece of poetry.'" We recognize this as a tombstone epitaph, yet hear it spoken as well. But who is talking? The father, the poet, speaks for the son, through the son, about both father and son, joined in their shared name. The son lies under the stone, where he is not only a boy but his father's "best piece of poetry." And as that he can continue to speak—of separation and diminishment, but of completion as well. Both Jonsons, merged in a name, become an inscription, which becomes a speaking voice, which becomes a line of poetry, a crucial moment in, perhaps, "his best poem." The pain of the poem, most desperately present in "O could I lose all father now! for why / Will man lament the state he should envy," turns into a final, tender creative act: "Rest ... and ... say ... " If this is small comfort, it is the best Jonson can offer himself. Jonson knows too well that man *will* "lament the state he should envy." What we believe fails to displace what we feel. Every time we will lament. And insofar as the poem contains this lament, Jonson's reanimation of his son will permit the boy to say only: Here I am; here you are. Although this is also: Here we both are.

The most telling points of comparison between Jonson's two poems are the moments of failed or achieved religious consolation. The presence of faith in "On My First Son" is enlarged, perhaps, by the awareness that the "just day" is the boy's birthday, and that father and son share the same name, "child of my right hand" being the literal translation of the Hebrew *Benjamin*. Or perhaps these are bitter, wounding ironies. In "Daughter," the father appears to accept that "all heaven's gifts" must eventually be returned. Even if we don't share Jonson's faith, we cannot doubt its potential force. But I don't think we feel that power operating in the poem—belief coming to rescue a man from pain. Tonally, the line, "It makes the father less to rue," feels breezy, and the syntax of the couplet—since x is true, y must follow—sounds like the bland beginning of a legal document: Having established that all gifts of heaven must be returned, the undersigned herewith forfeits any right to complain about the matter.

The moment that troubles me most, however, is the image of the child placed in Mary's "virgin-train." The poem asserts this as fact: to comfort the mother (who weeps, whereas the father merely rues) the Virgin Mary intercedes. We can accept this as a general article of faith, which all of the innocent are granted. But the poem, here resisting mere doctrine, chooses to present the act as singular, a result of heavenly sympathy for the *mother's* loss. Yet the moment is not shown as an actual revelation. Nor is it presented as an imaginative construct, contrived by a man acting as father, husband, and poet—invoking, even inventing, a vision of the afterlife to console his wife.

The next question would be: And why would he not require similar consolation? I can think of three answers. Because he doesn't care, the girl's death not having moved him deeply. Because his faith keeps him from being overwhelmed by loss. Or because he's trying to master his pain in order to help his wife. The first answer I want to reject; if the father simply doesn't care, that would trivialize what the poet eventually wrote. The second seems tangential to the poem's assertions. There is no evidence that Jonson's belief is stronger than his wife's, even if he does not weep. The third answer strikes me as the poem's most interesting *possibility*, which leads me to believe that Jonson failed to discover his best and most powerful subject.

The sign of this failure is that the poet is not sufficiently implicated in his poem. He gives himself the opportunity, but refuses to recognize it. The uneasy depiction of heaven is one sign of that refusal. But consider also the distance between husband and wife, and more importantly between father and poet. The father is not an "I" but "the father," an odd, uneasy generalization. The poem seems like an avoidance of the personal, but if so that avoidance is not an active feature of the poem. As a potential concern—and a rich and complicated one—emotional avoidance goes unrecognized. And yet the poem seems to want to move *toward* the personal: from "*the* father" to "*her* mother" to "*this* grave," to the final gesture of farewell. The poem travels from fact ("Here lies . . . ") and doctrine ("Yet all heaven's gifts . . . ") toward feeling.

But Jonson's "On My First Daughter" does not fail because it refuses to become sufficiently emotional; it fails because it does not discover and then utilize the emotional arc embedded within it. I take its truest *possible* subject to be a struggle between giving in to or holding back from potentially complicated feeling. In this sense, the "character" of the father is undeveloped, the attitude of the poet unclear, and the emotional life of the poem unexplored.

Although the ending of the poem—". . . cover lightly, gentle earth"—is more than merely sweet (and is arguably the poem's best moment), compare it to the concluding gesture of "On My First Son": "Rest in soft peace . . . " That poem, of course, doesn't end there. The available conceit (or call it a cliché, which it certainly is, if we remove the adjective "soft") generates a dazzling moment: ". . . and asked, say, 'Here doth lie / Ben Jonson . . . '" And when he discovered that turn, I imagine Jonson felt the pleasure of true accomplishment. Knowing such satisfaction did not call his grief into question; he went on working. That's good, he thought, that works.

At first all subjects are equal in their possibilities, although larger, more glamorous and more obviously consequential subjects will always seem particularly appealing.

But the political prisoner will not automatically write better or more significant poems than the middle-class American citizen. The struggle to survive oppression isn't a *better* subject than the fear of growing old or the death of a child. But since any subject is, by definition, a "topic' or "theme," it has yet to be located in those precise attitudes, tonalities, and images that will give it its necessary relationship to reality. The writer of either poems or criticism who feels that "the matter of thought" is sufficient forgets the attitude or "posture" that both statue and poem must be given to make them seem fully alive.

We cannot choose a wrong subject. If the primary danger is mistaking the subject for the poem itself, the practical risk is remaining too attached to any subject, and so frustrating the unfolding of an as-yet-unimagined poem. A poem triggered by a death may become a poem about that death. Or its true and most resonant subject may be discovered elsewhere—a quarrel with ourselves, with what we want to believe, or what we think we need to believe, in order to be ourselves. In life, any particular death may be crushing. In art, a death can serve as an occasion for wonderfully unpredictable realizations. The sense that a poem relates the true and immediate feelings of its author is one of poetry's most persuasive and most useful illusions.

Poetry and Consolation

"In the days right after September 11," a friend of mine said, "I didn't want to read, but I could listen to music." That made sense to me. Poetry demands concentration; music engulfs us. Poetry has to *say* things; music releases us from thought. Or music offers that illusion, which, for a while, may be what we need, the way when we're sad we listen to sad songs.

We don't want to feel worse, but we don't want to be cheered up either. Perhaps we want to be alone, but not completely. A song—and a poem as well, when we're ready for it—offers a kind of companionship, a connection with those who made from loss something complete and beautiful. Eventually art can do more. It can enlarge—then clarify—how we feel and act. But initially it gives us a shape that encloses its subject, a shape that, by extension, might surround and contain our own thoughts and feelings. This assertion of form—form before meaning—is art's first and most essential gesture of consolation.

Death dissolves form, and the deaths of September 11 left us vulnerable and imperiled. Suddenly chaos was real. We had to consider how the world we knew might survive. Would it survive? Art can't say the world will survive, of course, but art can suggest, through the example of its own shape, what we need. "The background in hugeness and confusion," Robert Frost writes in his essay about Edwin Arlington Robinson, "shading away from where we stand into black and utter chaos; and against the background any small man-made figure of order and concentration . . . how much more it is than nothing."

"After great pain, a formal feeling comes—," Emily Dickinson writes in a poem frequently mentioned as one people turned to, when they turned to poetry, after September 11. The poem's beauty is undeniable, as is the precision of its thinking, yet its severity and bleakness at first seem unlikely to appeal to anyone looking for comfort. Here is the complete poem:

> After great pain, a formal feeling comes—
> The Nerves sit ceremonious, like Tombs—
> The stiff Heart questions was it He, that bore,
> And Yesterday, or Centuries before?
>
> The Feet, mechanical, go round—
> Of Ground, or Air, or Ought—
> A Wooden way
> Regardless grown,
> A Quartz contentment, like a stone—
>
> This is the Hour of Lead—
> Remembered, if outlived,
> As Freezing persons, recollect the Snow—
> First—Chill—then Stupor—then the letting go—

How much closer to death can we get? That "letting go" is a person's last conscious moment. And yet—it can be "outlived," and return as memory. In this way, the meaning of "letting go" enlarges to attach itself to the poem's initial subject: great pain. The poem makes no promises. That "formal feeling" is like the literal moment of freezing. But it is only *like* it. And just as some who freeze are saved, so we may hope to outlive—and perhaps even let go of—great pain. Consolation appears through our recognition and awareness of metaphor.

Since great poetry can be complicated and difficult, it may not serve as well (or as immediately) as lesser work. W. H. Auden expressed some of the frustrations of the poet at this state. "It is a sobering experience," Auden writes,

> for any poet: to realize that it is not his work, not even the work of Dante or Shakespeare, that most people treasure as magic talismans in times of trouble, but grotesquely bad verses written by maiden ladies in local newspapers; that millions in their bereavements, heartbreaks, agonies, depressions, have been comforted and perhaps saved from despair by appalling trash while poetry stood helplessly and incompetently by.

So it's interesting that of all the poems circulated after September 11, the one that seems to have been most widely shared is a poem by Auden—"September 1, 1939." Beginning with the title, its relevance does seem uncanny. Here is the beginning of the first of the poem's nine stanzas:

> I sit in one of the dives
> On Fifty-Second Street
> Uncertain and afraid
> As the clever hopes expire
> Of a low and dishonest decade:

Waves of anger and fear
Circulate over the bright
And darkened lands of the earth,
Obsessing our private lives;
The unmentionable odour of death
Offends the September night.

And the stanza ends, "I and the public know / What all schoolchildren learn, / Those to whom evil is done / Do evil in return." But the most famous moment in this poem is the last line of its penultimate stanza: "We must love one another or die." I suspect that this is the gesture most eagerly seized upon in September of 2001. In the midst of chaos, who doesn't want to believe in the efficacy of love? But is the line true? Will we die if we do not love? Can love save us from death?

Auden himself became troubled. After the poem was published he declared that sentence "a damned lie," and he changed it to "We must love one another and die." Later, still unhappy, he eliminated the whole stanza. Finally he disowned the poem entirely, claiming that it was "infected with an incurable dishonesty."

Many have claimed that the initial revision of "or die" to "and die" makes the line more truthful. But the altered line seems to me less accurate, since even if we have to die, we are under no *obligation* to love. And Auden's first version does make sense if we provide certain qualifications. If we do not love one another in the biological sense we will, as a species, vanish. But that doesn't seem sufficient. Or we could turn to a religious explanation: that through love, death itself can be overcome. But those really aren't the terms of the poem. Finally, we could say that the line suggests we may actually die from the condition of being unable or unwilling to love. That's certainly true, I think, though it solves a problem by blurring a definition, which seems too much like figuring out a riddle. All of these readings feel like justifications rather than discoveries. Moreover, in the context of its stanza the line presents even more difficulties:

> All I have is a voice
> To undo the folded lie,
> The romantic lie in the brain
> Of the sensual man-in-the-street
> And the lie of Authority
> Whose buildings grope the sky:
> There is no such thing as the State
> And no one exists alone;
> Hunger allows no choice
> To the citizen or the police;
> We must love one another or die.

To me that colon after "sky" indicates that the statements that follow, however wise they may sound, should be taken as examples of romantic lies. "There is no such thing as the State." But there is. "And no one exists alone." But surely some do. And yet—from a different perspective the State might seem insubstantial and contrived, a fabrication, not a real "thing" at all. Similarly, no one can be said to live in complete isolation; no man, after all, is an island. So the statements contain competing and antithetical truths. Or lies, depending upon your point of view.

The next assertion is worrisome in the same way. At first it looks reasonable: the powerful and the powerless, the oppressor and the oppressed, are equally controlled by "hunger." However, to say that this allows neither any "choice" is to radically limit the ability of people to act—for good or ill—against such forces, as if we were driven only by our bodies. Nor does it seem fair to position the police so clearly against the citizen.

Finally, "We must love one another or die" presents itself as both a wise instruction and a romantic lie that needs to be exposed. When the poem seems most truthful, even most consoling, it is in fact most deceptive, most deeply ironic.

Taking the poem this way invites a sequential reading, as follows: We accept those four pronouncements first as the truth; then we recognize that they may be flawed, or ambiguous, or just plain wrong; and then, seeing this as the poem's intent, we realize we must confront—as the poem wants us to—our own assumptions, our desire for romantic lies, epigrammatic wisdom, and the easy consolations of affirmation. I like this reading. But I don't believe it.

First of all, Auden's revisions seem designed to make the lines more true, rather than more effectively ironic. Secondly, Auden was notoriously careless about punctuation, colons and semicolons in particular, and my argument asks a lot of that colon. On the other hand, these two arguments take the author's apparent intent too much into account, and every poet deserves to write a better poem than he thought he was writing. But the most powerful case against my interpretation is that nobody, in fact, reads the poem this way. Perhaps that's why Auden disowned it—because it didn't work. Or perhaps it was because he could never make it sufficiently true.

But *even so* I could hold on to my reading if I felt the poem itself—rather than the author, or the mass of previous readers—supported it. But I don't. I would feel my reading was an imposition upon an ambitious but conflicted poem, and I would find my thinking clever rather than revelatory. All of this may add up to little more than a curious textual problem. But I think it suggests what we want from poems—not just form and the enveloping semblance of sympathetic emotion (as in music, which of course poetry uses), but actual wisdom. After September 11, "September 1, 1939" was often spoken of as a "wise" poem. When I asked several fellow poets what they had turned to, or been sent, or read in articles, Auden's poem was almost always there. I won't hazard a guess as to how Auden would have felt about this.

Here is a much less well-known poem a friend showed me, by a writer I didn't know, a Polish poet named Tomasz Jastrun. The poem, translated by Daniel Bourne, was written at the beginning of the 1980s, after Soviet troops had occupied Afghanistan and, in response to the rising power of Solidarity, were threatening to invade Poland as well. The poem is called "Afghanistan":

> On the soldiers' shoulders
> Ride the white doves of peace
> With their eyes poked out
>
> As long as the Afghan people
> Are in need of help

The soldiers will remain
And remain and remain

We cry out
Butterflies and crickets in bondage
But who will understand
The language of butterflies and crickets

Those breathing freedom
Have a different set of problems
A shorter memory
They slip off to sleep untroubled
One day to wake up
In Afghanistan

Afghanistan is both a literal place and a state of mind, an awareness of danger and helplessness. Those who take freedom for granted have their own real problems, but they are also under less pressure to remember what does not immediately concern them. Their sleep is undisturbed until, one day, their world also changes.

The poem works as a metaphor, the essential stuff of poetry—seeing one thing in terms of something different. And metaphors, daringly employed, are not merely descriptive but demanding. The reader's response is an action that connects and uncovers, a discovery of relationship. Those who understand the Afghanistan of Jastrun's poem will be less able to sleep untroubled, knowing how fragile their own safety is.

The poem I would have chosen to share after September 11 is by another Polish poet, Tadeusz Różewicz. It's called "In the Middle of Life," or in some translations, "In the Midst of Life." Both versions of the title have useful reverberations. "In the midst of life we are in death" is from the Burial of the Dead in the *Book of Common Prayer.* "In the middle of my life I found myself in a dark wood" is the opening of Dante's *Inferno.* This is the beginning of Różewicz's poem as translated by Czesław Miłosz:

> After the end of the world
> after my death
> I found myself in the middle of life
> I created myself
> constructed life
> people animals landscapes
>
> this is a table I was saying
> this is a table
> on the table are lying bread a knife
> the knife serves to cut the bread
> people nourish themselves with bread
>
> one should love man
> I was learning by night and day
> what one should love
> I answered man

The death at the beginning of this poem isn't literal. That is, the poem is not interested in a visionary world. It's committed to this one, to the ways in which, after great pain or loss, our world needs to be reconstructed. I don't know if the poem is comforting. It is stabilizing. And its assertion of form is direct and essential. *This is,*

the poem says—a gesture that moves from observation
("this is a table") to declaration ("one should love man")
and halfway through the poem to moral judgment. (An
old woman leading a goat, Różewicz writes, is "more
necessary / and more precious / than the seven wonders
of the world," and whoever thinks she is not is "guilty
of genocide.") The poem ends with an act of connective
restoration in the face of God's silence:

> the man talked to the water
> talked to the moon
> to the flowers to the rain
> he talked to the earth
> to the birds
> to the sky
> the sky was silent
> the earth was silent
> if he heard a voice
> which flowed
> from the earth from the water from the sky
> it was the voice of another man

"Only the very greatest art," the novelist Iris Murdoch
has written, "invigorates without consoling." I wrote that
sentence down in my notebook years ago, and have often
wondered exactly what it means. Now I know.

And in the aftermath of September 11, I ended up
thinking about *King Lear*, a play that seems designed
to deny us solace, or cheer, or comfort. Having taken
the lives of nearly all of its characters, how can the play
invigorate, how can it fill its audience with life and energy? But it does. There's the beauty of its language, the

elegance of its form. True, but not enough. Great art, like *Lear*, changes the way we look at the world. It doesn't tell us what to think so much as it gives us the means to think more clearly. Clarity may not console, but it can exhilarate.

Art at its greatest doesn't work by convincing us of any particular idea—that we need to trust in love, for example, or that we need to reject the lies of love. Great art simply makes its subject more visible. That allows us to see the rest of the world more clearly. At least it gives us that chance, even if the world may still be no easier to bear, and death certainly no less enveloping.

September 11 was a kind of national death, out of which life needed to be reconstructed, "people animals landscapes." This is a table, the poet says. Begin with that. This is a window. This is a man.

"There is no consolation in tragedy," the novelist Milan Kundera has written. "Tragedy gives us an illusion of greatness and meaning." Happening upon Kundera's words recently I thought, That's right; there can be no consolation because there is illusion. Then I realized I'd just misread Kundera's sentence, that he had in fact written: "There *is* consolation in tragedy." And I thought, That's right, too. There is consolation because there is illusion. And I remembered blind Gloucester in *King Lear*. After the battle's lost, he doesn't want to get up and move on. "No further, sir," he tells his son Edgar, who's trying once again to save him. "A man may rot even here." And Edgar replies, "What, in ill thoughts again? Men must endure / Their going hence, even as their coming hither; / Ripeness is all: Come on." To which Gloucester says, "And that's true too." How like Shakespeare, in the greatest of all his tragedies, to follow a sweeping declaration of wisdom—"Ripeness is all"—with a modest qualification. How like Shakespeare to end his play with a moment— Lear's death—that feels like the bleakest irony, as well as the most improbable comfort. And which is a double illusion. The illusion that Lear hears Cordelia speak. The illusion that there is a Lear.

I want to end with a poem that seems to me successful in managing the kind of strategy I failed to convince myself was embodied by Auden's "September 1, 1939." By strategy I mean the use of wise statements that first appear true, then feel wrong, and then finally are corrected into a larger or different truth. The poem is Robert Frost's "Directive." It begins:

> Back out of all this now too much for us,
> Back in a time made simple by the loss
> Of detail, burned, dissolved, and broken off
> Like graveyard marble sculpture in the weather,
> There is a house that is no more a house
> Upon a farm that is no more a farm
> And in a town that is no more a town.

The journey we're encouraged to take is both literal (a walk in the woods) and symbolic (an exploration of the self). Our guide, we're informed, has at heart only our getting lost. But we need to be lost, and midway through the poem we're told:

> . . . if you're lost enough to find yourself
> By now, pull in your ladder road behind you

And put a sign up CLOSED to all but me.
Then make yourself at home.

How can we make ourselves at home when home is
exactly where we'd be if we weren't lost? Trust me, the
poem says, having announced its untrustworthiness. We
have arrived at what once was a home:

> First there's the children's house of make believe,
> Some shattered dishes underneath a pine,
> The playthings in the playhouse of the children.
> Weep for what little things could make them glad.

Then there's the house "that is no more a house . . . no
playhouse but a house in earnest." And near it a brook.
Our destination—and our destiny—is an old cedar at the
waterside, where, the speaker says,

> I have kept hidden in the instep arch . . .
> A broken drinking goblet like the Grail
> Under a spell so the wrong ones can't find it,
> So can't get saved, as Saint Mark says they mustn't.
> (I stole the goblet from the children's playhouse.)
> Here are your waters and your watering place.
> Drink and be whole again beyond confusion.

Wouldn't we like to believe in that: to be whole beyond confusion? To be whole *again*. Yet isn't that impossible in this world? Frost's final lines have the declarative
authority of "We must love one another or die." And
yet—our goblet is only *like* the Grail. And it was pilfered

from the children's playhouse. It's a make-believe Grail, and the wholeness we're promised is also make-believe. But that doesn't mean it's false. Since our journey has been made-up, should we expect anything but a make-believe truth? Moreover, Frost is very serious about make-believe. "Life sways perilously at the confluence of opposing forces," he writes in a letter in 1938. "Poetry in general plays perilously in the same wild place. In particular it plays perilously between truth and make-believe. It must be extravagant poetry to call it true make-believe—or making believe what is so."

This is our destination: making believe what is true—"any small figure of order and concentration." The last two lines of "Directive," a friend of mine said, are a kind of prayer. If so, they are the prayer of someone who suspects he has invented his belief. They are a prayer for the faithless who cannot relinquish the idea of faith. The poem sways perilously between certainty and homelessness, between the promise of revelation and the evidence of abandonment. And we who once were lost are meant to find ourselves, perilously—but not hopelessly—in the same wild place.

Poetry and Stupidity

1. Obscurity

One of the shortest and most provocative pieces in Paul Valéry's "A Poet's Notebook" reads, in its entirety:

> STUPIDITY AND POETRY. There are subtle relations between these two categories. The category of stupidity and that of poetry.

I can't recall when I first read this, but I remember thinking it was true. Also funny. Also like some Zen koan designed to knock me on the head. Was it true because it was so obviously untrue? Or because it seemed to provide no way to ascertain its truth? Or perhaps I just believed it because I didn't want to feel stupid.

That Valéry's equation didn't appear to make sense was a plus for me. Did it even want to make sense? A little further down the same page, I found:

> OBSCURITY, A PRODUCT OF TWO FACTORS. If my mind is richer, more rapid, freer, more disciplined than yours, neither you nor I can do anything about it.

This was spikier, more aggressively funny. Or maybe not funny at all. And obscurity, unlike ambiguity, somehow seemed connected to stupidity—how dumb you felt when you didn't get the joke.

2. Play

Setting aside the truth, Valéry's equation of poetry and stupidity is a brilliant provocation. But to what end? It feels like a riddle, which makes it a metaphor, or more precisely a simile: Poetry is like stupidity because . . . But no single answer appears to have been promised. Instead there are those "subtle relations," which someone with a rich, rapid, and disciplined mind might easily perceive.

But how to get even close to an answer? The most surprising word— "stupidity"—seems like the logical place to start. Had Valéry written of the subtle relations between ambiguity and poetry, we would not be surprised. It would appear obvious, ambiguity being one of poetry's tools. Had he spoken of confusion and poetry, we'd probably be intrigued, but not thrown off-balance. Surely poetry can use confusion as a strategy; let's hear more. But can it use stupidity? And have we already wandered from the central question, which was not *use* but *relationship*? After all, if stupidity consorts with subtlety, it changes into cunning. Or seems to.

To confuse matters further, "stupidity" is not Valéry's word, but the choice of his translator, Denise Folliot, in my edition of *The Art of Poetry* (Vintage, 1961). Valéry's word is "bétise," which he selected over the more seemingly appropriate "stupidité." My *Larousse* gives "foolish" as the primary meaning of "bétise," and it may be useful to follow the implications of "foolishness," which makes sense, even if it may make too much sense.

A poet fools around with words. And that's one way of getting a poem started—just playing, not asserting a concept or an idea, because as Valéry says (also in "A Poet's

Notebook"), "If you want to write verse and you begin with thoughts, you begin with prose." Redefining "stupidity" as "foolishness" feels both right and inadequate, as if the riddle's answer were too easy. On the other hand, are we looking for an answer, or are we trying to discover those elusive "subtle relations"? "The proper object of poetry," Valéry writes, becoming oracular again, "is what has no single name, what in itself provokes and demands more than one expression."

3. Foolishness

One of the appealing aspects of "foolishness" for me is the way it suggests a Shakespearean fool, that character who always has the cleverest, most difficult, and most profound lines: a poet, in other words, in disguise. I think particularly of Lear's fool.

Wordplay is the fool's essential weapon. His mind is richer, more rapid, freer, and more disciplined than Lear's, who commits the disasterously foolish act of dividing his kingdom, then exiling the one daughter who loves him. The fool is determined to make Lear aware of what he's done:

> FOOL: Nuncle, give me an egg and I'll give thee two crowns.
> LEAR: What two crowns shall they be?
> FOOL: Why, after I have cut the egg i' the middle and eat up the meat, the two crowns of the egg. When thou clovest thy crown i' the middle and gav'st away both parts, thou bor'st thine ass on thy back o'er the dirt.

Thou hadst little wit in thy bald crown
when thou gav'st thy golden one away.

(I.iv.148–156)

Riddles are one of the oldest forms of poetry, and
the fool's wit often reveals itself in riddle-like questions.
What are the two parts of an egg like? Answer: the king.
Who besides the fool is a fool? The king again. "Thou
hast pared thy wit o' both sides," the fool says, "and left
nothing i' the middle." (I.iv.177–178) This fooling around
is serious business, the stakes being the sanity of the king
and the fate of his kingdom, not to mention the life of
the fool.

Lear is distracted but not yet mad when his fool begins
to taunt him, licensed as the fool is to tell the truth, reluc-
tant as he is to tell it directly. Lear must see it for himself,
but the king doesn't care to play the fool's games. And yet
if he could engage in these riddles he would be thinking
metaphorically, which means seeing one thing in terms
of something else. His inability to see himself in terms of
someone else—Cordelia, for example—starts the ruinous
spiral of the play.

> LEAR: Who is it that can tell me who I am?
> FOOL: Lear's shadow.
>
> (I.iv.220–221)

If he could solve this, he might yet rescue himself.
"Lear's shadow" is both the answer to the question and
the way to find the answer. Lear has become the shadow
of himself, the fool suggests. But also, Lear's shadow, the

diminished thing, can still tell him who he is, just as that part of him who is the fool shadows Lear, and tells him who he is, and fails, and disappears from the play.

King Lear, we might say, is—in part—about the failure of metaphor, meaning the failure of art.

4. Blunders and Errors

My friend John, who knows French well, tells me that *stupidité* implies an utter lack of intelligence, whereas *bétise* is a sort of capacity to commit blunders or errors in judgment. Blunders and errors are intriguing when connected to poetry, though perhaps too much like fooling around. If the poet begins by playing with language, unaware of where the words might lead him, blunders and errors are inevitable. Or perhaps it's more accurate to think that at this point everything is blundering—fumbling around helplessly in the dark—in which case errors are actually impossible because no context exists in which to declare that any gesture should be called an error. There are only possibilities, some richer than others. There is only what might come next.

Not perceiving what might come next is important. To know too quickly the "idea" of the poem would be to lock it in place, to turn the process of composition into translation—how can this thought be expressed *poetically*? The poet must value *not* understanding, that kind of stupidity.

The poet must also know when to become smart. This begins with the discovery of the true subject of the poem, the surprise of recognizing what could not have been predicted. "In prose," Valéry writes, "one can draw up a plan and *follow* it!" In a poem the plan gets assembled as the poem comes into being, as the poet gradually becomes aware of where to go, which is where the language of apparent blunders and errors has been leading. The poet needs to be stupid, but also alert. There is a subtle relationship between these two categories.

The making of a poem is rarely a singular *act*, more often an extended *process*. At some point, alertness turns into an awareness of content as well as a certain range of possibilities and limitations. Once that context has been sensed, blunders and errors can be identified. The process of revision begins, even if at any moment the poem may need to be dismantled and re-envisioned.

5. Vacancy

It occurs to me that it is impossible to know what Valéry considers the subtle relations between poetry and stupidity. Of course there may be clues in the many essays of his I haven't read. But I like the idea of not knowing, even of imagining that Valéry had no idea what he meant. What's the point then? The point is the challenge to see what connections we might stumble over, then imagine. Valéry urges us to wander, *and* to be alert.

So there *is* a significant leap between *King Lear* and revision, but also an important connection. If Lear could revise himself, re-envision how he conceives of his relation to others, he might save himself and Cordelia. Yet I have no reason to believe Valéry was entertaining this line of thought. He could have been thinking about a

different play. He could have been thinking about dinner. Or a poem about a pear. The leap itself is what his lines urge us toward—less a particular idea than a way of arriving
at ideas.

As I've suggested, there's a usefulness to errors and blunders. First drafts are full of them. The point is not to try to avoid them, but to use them as ways of getting to the next, better sentence. The experienced writer is wary about applying critical intelligence too quickly. When linked to stupidity, the progression of a poem may involve a period of resonant vacancy. This can lead to an openness to chance, which might also serve as one definition of inspiration.

The excitement of writing a poem is not the following of a plan but the discovery of a subject. And I like to think of those discoveries as inspiration, an inspiration that doesn't precede the making of the poem, but is summoned into being by the poet's engagement with language—fooling around, and then being critical, and then fooling around again. Beginning poets need to learn how to be stupid. That is, they must find a way to embrace a kind of vacancy—we might call it daydreaming—that results in the acceptance of interesting language no matter where it might lead.

6. Surprise

In Valéry's remark on poetry and stupidity, what at first seemed like a problem—what sense does it make?—now feels like an opportunity, a prompt, a kind of assignment—*Connect these two words if you can*—which might lead to that state of receptivity out of which metaphors, and then poems, can be made.

But what about the reader? Fair enough to link poetry and poet, but does Valéry's claim make any sense if we connect poetry and reader? At first, no. Who wants a stupid reader? Or one with the inclination to commit errors of judgment. But what about a reader who values "vacancy," that reluctance to require too quickly the *meaning* of the poem, that awareness of the dangers of paraphrase? This reader allows the poem to be surprising, just as it once surprised the poet by revealing its content—just as we were surprised by Valéry's audacious linking of the high (poetry) and the low (stupidity).

Elsewhere in "A Poet's Notebook" Valéry wonderfully defines metaphor as "*what happens* when one *looks in a certain way*" (his emphasis). I've always valued the insistence on action here. Insofar as a metaphor *happens,* it is a dramatic moment, like an act a character in a play must perform—slam a door, un-sheath a dagger, rip off his own clothes—because of what he has been made to feel. Metaphor is a revelation of sensibility.

7. Order

But there is a third word in Valéry's remark—which, along with poetry and stupidity, is repeated twice—and that is "category" (*ordre*). So far I have emphasized the *process* of both writing and reading, and considered stupidity and poetry in this light. But "category" seems much more static and singular—a classification, a way of dividing a system into specific units. Linked by being part of a larger system, poetry and stupidity appear to be necessary to each other.

Poems, however, are different from poetry. They are its multiple parts. Moreover, poetry as a classification is always being redefined. It no longer corresponds, as it once seemed to, with "verse," which now carries a reduced sense of significance, and is often preceded by the word "light." Moreover, we usually speak of "free *verse*," but of "formal *poetry*," as if the formalists, being in power much longer, got to claim the more substantial word and so diminish the authority of their rivals.

To consider poetry as a category, a basic proposition might be to say that poetry is *a kind of writing, variously defined*. But in relation to Valéry this doesn't take us very far. What may be helpful is that sense of a "category" as being static, basic, knowable, one kind of thing, or one class of things. Interestingly, "category" is never given by the *Larousse* as a synonym for "*ordre*." Instead we are offered "class," but before that the more fluid "method," thus returning us to our earlier sense of process. And how much more sensible and less threatening—and less funny— Valéry's equation would be if translated as: "There are subtle relations between these two methods. The method of poetry and that of foolishness." Yes, we would say. Yes, there are.

However reasonable it may be to speak of the "category" of poetry, it seems rather comic to speak of the category of stupidity. There certainly are different kinds of stupidities, and perhaps they are even classifiable, but the prospect of trying seems enormously frustrating and— well—worthless. Could this be Valéry's aim: to make us stupid enough to try, and then smart enough to recognize our failure? To make us think and then defeat our thinking?

"Category" lends stupidity a kind of philosophical, or scientific, aura. To consider the idea of "category," then, is to raise the ante of the joke. But of course Valéry's lines don't add up to a joke because there is no punch line, therefore no conclusion, no answer, no resolution. It's as if, in the treacherous language of categories—of certainties that restrict and contain—Valéry only *pretends* to instruct us. Worrying about the value and meaning of the particular words he and his translator use both baffles and complicates the game.

8. Subversion

In his introduction to *The Art of Poetry*, T. S. Eliot writes that "Valéry is not primarily interested in teaching his readers anything. He is perpetually engaged in solving an insoluble problem—the puzzle of how poetry gets written." Even more than the solvable sense of *foolishness*, the resistant, blunt force of *stupidity*, along with *category*, combine to form an essential part of this insinuating if impossible puzzle.

Since every metaphor must break down at some point, by showing us the collision of stupidity and poetry Valéry creates a metaphor that seems already to have broken down. Our task is not to reassemble it, but to wonder about where trying to do so might lead us. Then how subversive might our thinking usefully become?

Teased into Thought: Three Endings

"The correction of prose," William Butler Yeats writes, "because it has no fixed laws, is endless, a poem comes right with a click like a closing box." But sometimes the ending of a poem can effectively surprise us by not clicking into place, by flattening itself out, swerving in another direction, or only pretending to end conclusively, or even by seeming to be the wrong sort of ending: opening that box, emptying its contents, and scattering them across the floor.

One of the most famous last lines in late twentieth-century American poetry is the end of James Wright's "Lying in a Hammock at William Duffy's Farm in Pine Island, Minnesota":

> Over my head, I see the bronze butterfly,
> Asleep on the black trunk,
> Blowing like a leaf in green shadow.
> Down the ravine behind the empty house,
> The cowbells follow one another
> Into the distances of the afternoon.
> To my right,
> In a field of sunlight between two pines,
> The droppings of last year's horses
> Blaze up into golden stones.
> I lean back, as the evening darkens and comes on.
> A chicken hawk floats over, looking for home.
> I have wasted my life.

Throughout the poem one might well be wondering: Where is Wright going? How is this accumulation of details going to add up? The poem does click into place, but at the same time seems to refuse to click into place, since we're allowed to read the last line in at least two radically different ways (unless, like Thom Gunn, we feel the last line "is certainly meaningless" and dismiss it). One response would emphasize sorrow—the speaker has indeed wasted his life, perhaps by failing to notice (as he does now) the world around him. But the poet is very careful to provide no backstory for the speaker. He hasn't suffered through a nasty divorce, or lost someone close to him, or realized, lying there in the hammock, that his politics, or his mean-spiritedness, or his alcoholism, have caused him to throw away what he should have cherished. He lies in that hammock and looks around, neither chastising himself nor revealing himself, except through the language that shows us what he sees.

The other way of reading the last line is positive: Thank God I have wasted my life, have spent my time paying attention to the world. In this reading, "wasted" includes the undertone of someone reproaching the speaker: Look at what you're doing, squandering your valuable time by lolling about and not being productive like the rest of us. But the speaker, having achieved a Zen-like sense of peace, would hardly agree, even if he were to hear this voice, even if he had been hearing this voice very clearly and thinking in response: Thank God I haven't been like the rest of you.

The details of the poem are beautiful in a particularly transformative way: the butterfly becomes "bronze," and yet its apparent solidity and statue-like permanence is belied by the way, asleep, it is "blowing like a leaf in green shadow." The cowbells are detached from the cows, as if only the sound were moving off "into the distances of the afternoon." And most notably, the horse droppings "blaze up into golden stones." Through alchemy, excrement is turned into gold; what was worthless has become precious. Or else: what was seemingly worthless always possessed value if one looked closely enough. The "alchemy," of course, consists of the observations of the poet transformed into evocative language. In this way the poem itself may become an object of great value or an emblem of wasted time—depending upon who is doing the looking and making the judgment.

The only moment in this sequence of images that seems infused with emotion belongs to that chicken hawk "looking for home." But even here the poem's doubleness checks any reductive response. What is the value of "home"? Is the bird looking for it with a kind of wistfulness? Has "home" become lost? Should we consider any kind of desperation? Or is the bird just "looking," as the speaker has been just looking. Then the bird floats above him, knowing full well where home is and when it will be time to return there.

Or should we see this moment as applying most of all to the speaker who is, after all, not home but at William Duffy's farm? Perhaps the speaker is yearning for a home that has been denied to him, or lost through time or circumstance. On the other hand, he may be perfectly comfortable, leaning back as the hawk floats above him, waiting for the evening to darken further until it will be time to go inside, and then perhaps head home.

All of this supports the radical ambiguity of the final line, which is, in its way, shocking. "I have wasted my life" apparently comes out of nowhere, either clicking everything into place, or opening everything up. Or both. The line seems to be a direct assertion of emotion. It removes us from what we have been seeing and places us inside the speaker's feelings. And yet we cannot be sure what his feelings are. All of the details seem to be clues that can be read in different ways, leading us to confront a lost, or a happy, man.

I can imagine some readers, like Thom Gunn, finding all of this pretentious and annoying—why doesn't he just tell us how he's feeling? As Gunn writes, "Other general statements of different import could well be substituted for [the last line] and the poem would neither gain nor lose strength." I can also imagine other readers feeling secure in their sense of the emotional state of the speaker at the end of the poem. Perhaps these readers have not experienced any ambiguity, or have discovered aspects of the poem that remain invisible to me, or have read into the poem biographical information that I do not know and would choose not to know. In other words, I am happy being able to imagine two quite different readings and allowing them to exist together without, as John Keats says, "any irritable reaching after fact and reason."

"Lying in a Hammock . . . " may be a useful example of Keats's conception of "negative capability" as applied to the reader. That is, I want to read the poem as encouraging us to remain in uncertainties and doubts, which means not trying to "solve" the poem but allowing ourselves to accept it, as if it were saying, Life is like this, isn't it? At the same time the poem refuses to clarify—or pin down—what "this" may be. (Or, as C. P. Cavafy writes, "A state of feeling is true and false, possible and impossible at the same time, or rather by turns.") The speaker leans back; the hawk floats above him. Home is somewhere, maybe close by, but just not here. Perhaps the way he has wasted his life floats from one truth to another, or one falsehood to another truth.

I suggested earlier that a possible strategy for the construction of a successful ending is to pretend that it is not a successful ending. Wright's last line in many ways fits this idea, though I have no idea whether Wright considered anything like that when composing the poem. Wright's ending sounds conclusive, but it isn't. It reverberates back through the poem, yet those reverberations are ambiguous. They don't lead us to the security of home, or to the specificity of a wasted life.

To pursue the effect of certain kinds of endings I want now to look at two very different poems with two very different endings, which I think, closely attended to, are similar in many ways. The ending of the first poem, Keats's "Ode on a Grecian Urn," is highly rhetorical. The ending of the second poem, Elizabeth Bishop's "Santarém," seems flat, diffident, off-handed, altogether devoid of the high drama and aggressive truth-telling of Keats's "Urn."

Keats's ending—"Beauty is truth, truth beauty,—that is all / Ye know on earth, and all ye need to know"—is often detached from the poem and embraced as a statement of great wisdom, as if to be wise like this were the ultimate aim of poetry. But seen closely in context, the ending poses at least as many problems as Wright's. Here is Keats's complete poem:

Ode on a Grecian Urn

I.

Thou still unravish'd bride of quietness,
    Thou foster-child of silence and slow time,
Sylvan historian, who canst thus express
    A flowery tale more sweetly than our rhyme:
What leaf-fring'd legend haunts about thy shape
    Of deities or mortals, or of both,
        In Tempe or the dales of Arcady?
    What men or gods are these? What maidens loth?
What mad pursuit? What struggle to escape?
        What pipes and timbrels? What wild ecstasy?

II.

Heard melodies are sweet, but those unheard
    Are sweeter; therefore, ye soft pipes, play on;
Not to the sensual ear, but, more endear'd,
    Pipe to the spirit ditties of no tone:
Fair youth, beneath the trees, thou canst not leave
    Thy song, nor ever can those trees be bare;
        Bold lover, never, never canst thou kiss,
Though winning near the goal—yet, do not grieve;
    She cannot fade, though thou hast not thy bliss,
        For ever wilt thou love, and she be fair!

III.

Ah, happy, happy boughs! that cannot shed
    Your leaves, nor ever bid the Spring adieu;
And, happy melodist, unwearied,
    For ever piping songs for ever new;
More happy love! more happy, happy love!
    For ever warm and still to be enjoy'd,
        For ever panting, and for ever young;
All breathing human passion far above,
    That leaves a heart high-sorrowful and cloy'd,
        A burning forehead, and a parching tongue.

IV.

Who are these coming to the sacrifice?
    To what green altar, O mysterious priest,
Lead'st thou that heifer lowing at the skies,
    And all her silken flanks with garlands drest?
What little town by river or sea shore,
    Or mountain-built with peaceful citadel,
        Is emptied of this folk, this pious morn?
And, little town, thy streets for evermore
    Will silent be: and not a soul to tell
        Why thou art desolate, can e'er return.

V.

O Attic shape! Fair attitude! with brede
    Of marble men and maidens overwrought,
With forest branches and the trodden weed:

Thou, silent form, dost tease us out of thought
As doth eternity: Cold Pastoral!
    When old age shall this generation waste,
    Thou shalt remain, in midst of other woe
Than ours, a friend to man, to whom thou say'st,
    "Beauty is truth, truth beauty,—that is all
        Ye know on earth, and all ye need to know."

The final two lines of this ode have been variously interpreted as a serious flaw in an otherwise beautiful poem, since it is a statement that is untrue or meaningless ("simple incomprehensibility," Ivor Winters asserts), or as a key to the poem's profound insights ("the wisdom of Keats's own widest experience of life," Aileen Ward writes). But as a clue to the poem's overall meaning, "Beauty is truth, truth beauty" may well be usefully considered as what Cleanth Brooks calls "a consciously riddling paradox." Therefore, what appears to be paradoxically meaningless may be taken as a strategy rather than an error. Now we should consider T. S. Eliot's response, which is reservedly and insightfully confused: ". . . this line strikes me as a serious blemish on a beautiful poem, and the reason may be either that I fail to understand it, or that it is a statement which is untrue . . . or perhaps the fact that it is grammatically meaningless conceals another meaning from me."

I like the idea that behind the appearance of the meaningless, another meaning—or more than one—may be concealed. Moving in this direction would cause us to ask what happens to our interpretation if the urn's statement is seen as true to the total drama of the poem precisely because it does not and is not intended to make sense. Therefore the *effect* of the apparent paradox may be more important than its meaning, or its meaning may lie in its effect. The reader's struggle to understand what Eliot understandably fails to understand reveals, through the intellectual drama of the struggle itself, those meanings that Eliot senses may have been concealed from him.

But those who would shy away from what seems intentionally meaningless might turn to Keats for help. In a letter of 1817 Keats seems to settle the matter by writing, "What the imagination seizes as beauty must be truth . . . " The urn's statement thus becomes Keats's statement, and as such can be understood (and qualified) by other ideas attributable to Keats. But the attentive reader is always careful not to be too quick to conflate poet and speaker, and in "Grecian Urn" we have a speaker (the urn) within a speaker (Keats), *or* a speaker (the urn) within a speaker (the voice who may or may not be *wholly* Keats) within an author (Keats, who invisibly controls everything). In the spirit of negative capability, Keats himself either settles or complicates the matter when he writes that "the camelion Poet . . . has no Identity" and is continually "filling some other Body." "Not one word I ever utter," Keats writes, "can be taken for granted as an opinion growing out of my identical nature—how can it, when I have no nature? . . . even now I am perhaps not speaking from myself: but from some character in whose soul I now live."

But before we pursue further the values and beauties of uncertainty, there is an important textual issue to confront. Who actually speaks the last two lines of the poem?

When old age shall this generation waste,

Thou shalt remain, in midst of other woe
Than ours, a friend to man, to whom thou say'st,
  "Beauty is truth, truth beauty,—that is all
    Ye know on earth, and all ye need to know."

Of course it's clear that it's the urn (meaning the voice Keats has invented for the urn) that offers us the consolatory advice about beauty and truth. But who is responsible for the rest of the ending? One possibility is the urn itself, in which case "ye" becomes us, and the equation of beauty and truth becomes both all that we know in life and all that we need to know, which at a glance would seem to be (as T. S. Eliot puts it) "untrue." We know and need to know more than this.

Another possibility is that the speaker of the poem (maybe Keats, maybe not) is responding, rather critically, to the urn's (or Keats's, or maybe not Keats's) formulation. The equation of beauty and truth is all that *the urn* in its beautiful pastoral silence knows and can know and therefore needs to know. This is as far as art goes. Beyond that lies, on the one hand, the "eternity" that teases us out of thought, and on the other hand, "breathing human passion," which is the life—*within the poem*—that undercuts the truth of the urn's pronouncement.

This qualification is appealing, because it allows the poem to end on a reassuringly sensible note. Art—in which beauty can become truth as it cannot in human life—is important precisely because of its difference from human life. So it need know no more. It need tell us nothing but what it is as itself. Beauty requires no justification. This reading is compelling in the way that it solves the logical and grammatical problems of the poem, but unconvincing in that it seems *only* to solve those problems, and in a rather clumsy way. To view the speaker as turning his back on the urn's statement is to drastically weaken the cumulative drama of the poem, and to reduce a complicated pattern of shifting experience to a philosophical quibble. If the urn can be profound but pretentious, the speaker's response seems both sensible and tonally snarky—That's all *you* know, urn.

Unfortunately we cannot be sure who Keats meant to be speaking. The first published version of the ode, in the *Lamia* volume of 1820, has quotation marks only around "Beauty is truth, truth beauty," but four transcripts of the poem survive and these, which may claim greater authority than the two original printings, omit any quotation marks at all in the final two lines. If we go with the transcripts, as I would, we complicate matters the most (as I would like to), since the identity of the speaker can only be determined by tone and attitude, rather than by punctuation. I can't say this is what Keats *intended*, but it seems likely that it's what a "camelion poet" might find attractive: the maximum amount of doubt and uncertainty. But if so, why? Again, as we asked of James Wright, why not be clear?

I want to suggest that the poem only *seems* to end by revealing its Truth, that in fact it is *designed* to baffle us, to leave us teased out of thought, and eventually *into* thought. I want to suggest an equation between the relationship of the urn and the speaker of the poem, and the poem itself and the reader. The speaker of the ode is returned to his "sole self" by the realization that the urn's beauty and enforced sense of timelessness has teased him out of thought. Or he has allowed this, even desired it, imagining eternity not as a cold pastoral, but the imminence of a warm embrace—"happy love . . . still to be enjoy'd."

Just as the ode's speaker has been drawn into the imagined life of the landscape pictured on the urn, so we have been engaged by the poem about the urn—charmed, beguiled, instructed, and finally baffled—or left, as Eliot would have it, with the sense of meaning hovering behind meaninglessness. Through the strategic use of paradox, the poem intentionally deceives us, or to be more precise, allows us to deceive ourselves. And why? If the enchantment of a work of art, at the moment of our most intense involvement, might seem to unite both heard and unheard music, both warmth and cold, both life and death and truth *and* beauty, Keats suggests that we must, living as we do in a world of human passion, save ourselves from the temptations of eternity, which are replicated in the enchantments of art.

Art is in love with itself, with its own form and being. Such self-love might convince the enraptured viewer of the urn (or reader of the poem) that there exists a beauty that is equal only to truth, all that art can and need know, and, for a moment, all that we need to know. But only for a moment. The imagination cannot cheat so well. Keats has risked incoherence to tell us this. Or rather, the poem does not *tell us* this. It enacts its meanings, so that our best responses are ones of discovery rather than mere assent. The poem about the urn becomes the poem of our experience, of the mind's experience. As Keats writes, "We read fine things but never feel them to the full until we have gone the same steps as the author."

Though in many ways as different as two poems can be, both "Lying in a Hammock . . ." and "Ode on a Grecian Urn" court meaninglessness. Elizabeth Bishop's "Santarém" may seem like an unlikely third in this trio, in that it appears (especially in its ending) to espouse neither the apparent mystery (or confusion) of "I have wasted my life," nor the apparent profundity (or confusion) of "Beauty is truth, truth beauty." One might be tempted to say that Bishop's poem is "pretty" rather than "beautiful," appealing rather than profound, comfortable rather than demanding. But if so one would be mistaken.

All three poems require reconsideration from the attentive reader, who may initially be unaware that any such demands have been made. All three invite the reader to *under-read*—or even *misread*—the poem, so that an interpretive correction would appear appropriate, and even necessary, to avoid ideas that are insufficient to the poem's complexity.

Elizabeth Bishop's "Santarém" ends with this pleasing and seemingly modest anecdote:

> In the blue pharmacy the pharmacist
> had hung an empty wasps' nest from a shelf:
> small, exquisite, clean matte white,
> and hard as stucco. I admired it
> so much he gave it to me.
> Then—my ship's whistle blew. I couldn't stay.
> Back on board, a fellow-passenger, Mr. Swan,
> Dutch, the retiring head of Philips Electric,
> really a very nice old man,

who wanted to see the Amazon before he died, asked, "What's that ugly thing?"

Mr. Swan's statement—a question of course, but really a condemnation—ends the poem, but suggests what the reader's response should be: No, it's not ugly, it's beautiful, because the poet finds it beautiful and therefore so do I, and so you, Mr. Swan, must be wrong! Or perhaps we don't get so worked up and just dismiss Mr. Swan with a shrug. He is, after all, an industrialist ("the retiring head of Philips Electric"), though on the other hand he has a beautiful name. And he wants to see the Amazon before he dies. This is a simple fact, but also a detail that could typecast Mr. Swan as either a capitalist tourist or an inveterate romantic.

But there is also Bishop's intervention: he is "really a very nice old man." This seems to ward off criticism, but at the same time feels defensive: he's nice—*really*, he is— even though we're about to see how wrong he is about the wasps' nest. But is he wrong? Or are we wrong to assume that he's wrong? This is the trap of the poem. But to examine how it works—how it clicks into place while seeming to float off the page—we must go back to earlier moments. Here is the complete poem:

Santarém

Of course I may be remembering it all wrong
after, after—how many years?

That golden evening I really wanted to go no
  farther;

more than anything else I wanted to stay awhile
in that conflux of two great rivers, Tapajós,
    Amazon,
grandly, silently flowing, flowing east.
Suddenly there'd been houses, people, and lots of
    mongrel
riverboats skittering back and forth
under a sky of gorgeous, under-lit clouds,
with everything gilded, burnished along one side,
and everything bright, cheerful, casual—or so it
    looked.
I liked the place; I liked the idea of the place.
Two rivers. Hadn't two rivers sprung
from the Garden of Eden? No, that was four
and they'd diverged. Here only two
and coming together. Even if one were tempted
to literary interpretations
such as: life/death, right/wrong, male/female
—such notions would have resolved, dissolved,
    straight off
in that watery, dazzling dialectic.

In front of the church, the Cathedral, rather,
there was a modest promenade and a belvedere
about to fall into the river,
stubby palms, flamboyants like pans of embers,
buildings one story high, stucco, blue or yellow,
and one house faced with *azulejos,* buttercup yellow.
The street was deep in dark-gold river sand
damp from the ritual afternoon rain,
and teams of zebus plodded, gentle, proud,
and *blue*, with down-curved horns and hanging ears,

pulling carts with solid wheels.
The zebus' hooves, the people's feet
waded in golden sand,
dampened by golden sand,
so that almost the only sounds
were creaks and *shush, shush, shush.*

Two rivers full of crazy shipping—people
all apparently changing their minds, embarking,
disembarking, rowing clumsy dories.
(After the Civil War some Southern families
came here; here they could still own slaves.
They left occasional blue eyes, English names,
and *oars.* No other place, no one
on all the Amazon's four thousand miles
does anything but paddle.)
A dozen or so young nuns, white-habited,
waved gaily from an old stern-wheeler
getting up steam, already hung with hammocks
—off to their mission, days and days away
up God knows what lost tributary.
Side-wheelers, countless wobbling dugouts . . .
A cow stood up in one, quite calm,
chewing her cud while being ferried,
tipping, wobbling, somewhere, to be married.
A river schooner with raked masts
and violet-colored sails tacked in so close
her bowsprit seemed to touch the church

(Cathedral, rather!). A week or so before
there'd been a thunderstorm and the Cathedral'd

been struck by lightning. One tower had
a widening zigzag crack all the way down.
It was a miracle. The priest's house right next door
had been struck, too, and his brass bed
(the only one in town) galvanized black.
Graças a deus—he'd been in Belém.

In the blue pharmacy the pharmacist
had hung an empty wasps' nest from a shelf:
small, exquisite, clean matte white,
and hard as stucco. I admired it
so much he gave it to me.
Then—my ship's whistle blew. I couldn't stay.
Back on board, a fellow-passenger, Mr. Swan,
Dutch, the retiring head of Philips Electric,
really a very nice old man,
who wanted to see the Amazon before he died,
asked, "What's that ugly thing?"

The poem begins with a wonderfully sneaky dis-
claimer: everything that follows may be wrong. After all,
how many years has it been? The question is unanswered,
replaced by memory—a single "golden evening," when
the speaker wished to "stay awhile / in that conflux of
two great rivers ... " Everything she can see around her is
"bright, cheerful, casual—or so it looked." Perhaps everything is only seemingly casual and cheerful. Perhaps
beneath or beyond the way something looks there is more
to see and to understand.

One of Bishop's important strategies in many of her
poems is correction. She often questions and then re-

considers what she's just said, which I want to read as an invitation for the reader to do the same. Here the two rivers she can see remind her of the two rivers that had "sprung / from the Garden of Eden," a nice literary leap. But wrong. There were four, and they went in different directions, whereas here they are coming together. Having invoked the literary, she casually extends it: perhaps one would be tempted to turn to literary "interpretations," for example: "life/death, right/wrong, male/female." But if so, such "notions" would resolve and dissolve into something beautifully philosophical: a "watery, dazzling dialectic." Has the word "dialectic" ever been so slyly imported into a poem? Have the dichotomies of life/death, etc., ever been seriously presented as "literary interpretations"? Oh well, says the poem, in any case I'm not really "tempted" in that direction. The Garden of Eden just popped into my mind. Or that's what I remember, which, of course, may be wrong.

The poem both appeals to and shrugs off literary and philosophical interpretations, as if to say, Go ahead, if that's the sort of thing you're interested in, I'm more interested in the sights. And so the poem moves to another place and another correction: "In front of the church, the Cathedral, rather . . . " This is repeated two stanzas later—"(Cathedral, rather!)"—the force of the exclamation mark playing nicely off the modesty of the parentheses. What, after all, is important?

Before we arrive at the blue pharmacy in the final stanza, and following the detour into literary interpretations, most of the poem consists of appreciative, anecdotal, descriptive wandering. There are "poetic" moments ("The street was deep in dark-gold river sand / damp from the ritual afternoon rain . . . "), and bits of information as well; it's as if someone had asked, for example, What happened in the Amazon after the Civil War? Were there slaves? And yes: "After the Civil War some Southern families / came here; here they could still own slaves." Then there are nuns, a cow, a river schooner, a story about lightning hitting that church (No—Cathedral!), and the priest who was saved because he wasn't there. After that she enters the "blue pharmacy" (what a strange and lovely way to describe it!) in which the speaker admires the "small, exquisite" wasps' nest, and is given it as a present. (Why a wasps' next should be in a pharmacy is not explained—it's just there. Should there be a reason?) This brings us back to Mr. Swan and what I have described as the "trap" of the poem.

It's a trap because Bishop has made it relatively (but not altogether) easy for us to condemn Mr. Swan—nice man that he is—as incapable of appreciating beauty. Now we may turn back to that "dazzling dialectic" Bishop has cannily embedded in the poem's second stanza. Thesis: the wasp's nest is beautiful ("exquisite" as the speaker says); Antithesis: the wasps' nest is "ugly," according to Mr. Swan, the man with the beautiful name. Since these seem to be dichotomies like "right/wrong, male/female" (both of which deserve to be applied to the poem), is there a synthesis to complete the dialectic? The poem provides none. Making the connection, if we choose to do so, is up to us.

But first we must realize that oppositions like ugly/ beautiful are inadequate, although a synthesis is possible, and potentially dazzling. This problem presents itself only after we've recognized that the poem is more than merely anecdotal, or merely beautiful. To *rescue* ourselves from that assumption we have to realize that we've been lured into asking the wrong question. The issue is not either/or. The issue is context. The wasps' nest is "exquisite" inside the blue pharmacy. On board the ship, even if the poet continues to find it beautiful (and we don't know that she does, since she never responds to Mr. Swan's remark), is it fair to criticize Mr. Swan for dismissing the wasps' nest as ugly? After all it is a *wasps' nest*, not the bust of Apollo.

What Mr. Swan's remark disproves is nothing less than the contention that truth is beauty. The word "wasp" comes with the implication of danger; and the word "nest" may suggest the imminence of such hidden danger. The word "swan," on the other hand, brings elegant love-liness to mind. But the issue here is not wasp/swan, just as it isn't beauty/ugliness, or any of those other reductive "literary" dichotomies.

But the "trap" of the poem involves our inevitable in-clination to judge; we can't help but form opinions. And this may reflect a more consequential misunderstanding of appearances. So Bishop's ending opens into a genuine dialectical problem, the solution to which is suggested by Wallace Stevens:

> They said, "You have a blue guitar,
> You do not play things as they are."
>
> The man replied, "Things as they are
> Are changed upon the blue guitar."

When Bishop accepts the wasps' nest as a gift, she removes it from its home and turns it into a souvenir, or an art object. But does the exquisite appearance of the nest depend upon its location and the first moment of seeing? Wrenched from these, surely it's understandable that the object might lose its aura and seem like a mere "ugly thing."

But what's more important is that Bishop chooses not to respond to Mr. Swan in her poem. He has the last word. When Bishop's fish in "The Fish" becomes as beautiful as a rainbow, she throws it back into the life-giving water. Here, in a more complicated maneuver, she turns that action over to us. And if we free ourselves from the easy response—agreement with the poet's apparent taste and judgment—we are moved into a more difficult dialectic, one in which we must reconsider the nature of our response as well as the complications of the poem.

Such a reconsideration should result in a redefinition of the poem's ambitions, even if we don't find a comfortable resolution. How much uncertainty are we prepared to accept without any irritable reaching after fact or reason—without demanding that Wright make it clear how he has wasted his life, without requiring Bishop to defend her possession of the wasps' nest, without asking Keats to admit to and then explain his paradoxes? When one river flows into another, at what point do they become the same river? When one idea confronts another, how can they be reconciled?

All three of these poems ask such questions. They do so by putting a great deal of pressure on their endings, though in each case their strategy is to pretend otherwise. With Wright and Keats we may immediately feel we understand the import and significance of their final gestures—until we think harder and look more closely. With Bishop, it's the rather surprising "incompletion" of her ending that forces us back through her anecdotal sightseeing to those "literary" conceptions that help us redefine and extend the substance of the poem.

In each case the reader is intentionally persuaded to be inattentive. So misreading is an occasion for correction. And correction is an occasion for discovery. Moreover, the stakes are high indeed: eternity, truth, beauty, love, life and death. These words may seem most applicable to Keats's ode, but Wright's poem is deeply committed to the vagaries of beauty and the consequences of a wasted (or a rich) life. And Bishop's poem is equally committed to the apprehension of beauty and what may lie behind the visible. The way the immediacy of the world—and of the poem—change how we look are among the most consequential concerns of all three poems, although, of course, we may say this of all good and great poems. So the apparent dichotomy of poet/reader is absorbed into the clarity of shared recognition. Beauty becomes truth.

2

In a Different Hour: Collaboration, Revision, and Friendship

Many years ago—and I really don't want to remember exactly how young we were—Stephen Dunn, a friend but not yet a collaborator, was traveling from New Jersey to Yaddo, the artists' colony in Saratoga Springs, New York. He stopped for the night at our house. During the course of the evening I recall bemoaning the fact that I hadn't written a poem—maybe not even tried to write one—in over a year. I had writer's block, I announced, as if it were an identifiable disease. I had not yet learned the wisdom of William Stafford's famous—or infamous—remark that there is no such thing as writer's block; all you have to do is lower your standards.

Of course Stafford didn't mean you ultimately aim for less. You just have to give yourself a break to get started, and accept whatever occurs to you because "something always occurs" to us, as Stafford says in his essay "A Way of Writing." Let the act of writing carry you beyond your first inevitably dull words to better words, better sentences that may give you access to something waiting in your mind "ready for sustained attention." This is the writer's daily work—putting some words down, then rearranging them, adding, subtracting, looking for a shape, a focus, "the poem's informing principle," as Stephen Dunn puts it in his essay "The Good, the Not So Good." If that's inspiration—and I like to think so—it's *earned* by the work of writing, not given as a gift of the gods like an autumn leaf fluttering down significantly on the poet's head.

These are some of the things I didn't know when

Stephen and I and my wife, Judy, were having dinner. "Writer's block blah blah blah," I continued. (I was about to spend some time at Yaddo also, arriving a few days after Stephen.) "Well," Stephen said amiably, "when you get to Yaddo, do what I do—write a new poem every day." I didn't know Stephen did this; the idea seemed inconceivable, even appalling. "I can't do that," I declared. "Yes you can," Stephen said. "But how?" "You just do it."

I knew that was true, but what a strange truth. You tell yourself to do it and you just do it. So I followed Stephen's advice, and that summer we started showing each other a new poem each day. Over the years, we developed rules. We could continue to revise a poem, but only for another day, to avoid getting stuck on it. Then a harder rule: a draft of the poem had to be done by lunchtime.

Of course almost all poets need trustworthy readers, but we were compressing the process radically. After lunch we'd work more on the poem, play tennis, then have drinks and show each other what we'd done, then work some more, and maybe look at the poems again later in the evening.

At times what I'd come up with by noon was something I could see promise in, even believe was already a poem. Most often, whatever we had at those moments were pieces of language that were just beginning to assert their power over us, just starting to ask to be honored as "poems." In daily life they would have found their way into the manila folder called "Notes," and perhaps languished there. But in those weeks at Yaddo, it was all work in progress at its earliest and most perilous state. Later I often couldn't believe I'd shown Stephen the mess I'd cobbled together that morning. But we learned how to manage these moments, what to be particular about, what to suggest, and how to find opportunity in the apparently incoherent. "This poem," I recall Stephen saying many times, "needs to make another move. Maybe halfway through." "What sort of move?" I'd ask, and he'd usually say he didn't know; that it was, after all, my poem. "Just go somewhere else."

Infuriating as this advice could be, it's stayed with me as a writer and as a teacher. When you think you're stuck, I tell my students, just go somewhere else. You believe your poem is about this beggar on the streets of Manhattan, but maybe he's there only to take you to a different place. So after the line about his raggedy pants (or maybe before that rather pallid line) write: "Meanwhile, in Argentina . . ." Why Argentina? Because you haven't been there. But if you don't like South America, go to Paris, or back to the room you lived in as a child, the one with the monsters in the closet, the one you had to leave when your parents divorced, and you cried, or refused to cry— whatever the poem needs.

Yet how easy it can be at noon at Yaddo (or The Mac-Dowell Colony, our other haven), and at such an early, tender moment in the life of the poem, to be dismissive, or know-it-all, or the opposite: too full of a kind of praise that hasn't yet been earned, inattentive to the wildness the poem might only have begun to hint at. We learned to be *appropriately* critical, meaning helpful, respectful of the whole endeavor, but insistent as well. Maybe once a summer at noon Stephen would read a poem, nod, and say, "Yes, you got it." How much better my sandwich tasted after that.

That first summer at Yaddo after my "writer's block," I wrote twenty-nine poems in as many days. Stephen probably wrote the same, maybe more. (Sometimes he'd sneak in a really short one to make the numbers add up.) But it was good to be competitive, as is inevitably the case with me and Stephen. In the afternoons we played tennis. Stephen always won. Sometimes I'd suggest his victory was a sign that my poem that morning was better. He'd say it was my turn to buy a new can of balls for tomorrow's game.

I think of this as "collaboration" rather than just "criticism" because of how quickly our poems would confront each other's sensibilities, how much we would risk, and how much we would borrow, or steal, from each other. "You can't write a serious poem about space aliens," Stephen once declared, suggesting that what I'd done that morning was doomed. But I kept on and yes, Stephen finally said, "You got it." Years later he also wrote a successful poem about space aliens, which I was very critical of for a long time.

We'd try to make things harder (or more playful) for each other by coming up with assignments—some we'd both do, some designed for the other person. Here are two short ones Stephen gave me a few years back: (1) Write the poem that can't be written; (2) Write a poem called "Against Compassion." I did both. The second ended up being called "Against Compassion," and the first "The Poem That Can't Be Written." And here's an assignment from Stephen that I couldn't do: Write a poem in which every fourth line obstructs where the poem appears to be going. Great assignment; too much math.

Sometimes, when we failed to get into a colony together, we'd find other ways of meeting for a couple of weeks. Once I rented a house outside Peterborough since Stephen had gotten into MacDowell and I hadn't. Sometimes we'd e-mail each other from home, making sure we responded as quickly as possible. For a while we sent each other lines from our own earlier poems that hadn't worked out—to be used, changed, or ignored. Every so often I'll see a poem of Stephen's and think, Isn't that a line I wrote fifteen years ago? It pleases me to wonder, as if it were evidence of another self I didn't know I had.

We also published a chapbook of "actual" collaborations called *Winter at the Caspian Sea,* poems in which we wrote alternate lines, folding the paper over so that only the second of the two lines could be seen, in the manner of the Surrealists' "Exquisite Corpse" game. Everything was done quickly, and no revisions were permitted. Our aim was to allow for as many surprises as possible. Another collaborative method we tried was designed this way: Each of us would write four lies (and yes, that's "lies," not "lines"), one of which had to be more elaborate than the others, on an agreed-upon subject. We could each use either one's list, but we gave ourselves only fifteen minutes to write the poem. Why lies? To avoid the ordinary, to move the material as quickly as possible into metaphorical territory. One pair of these poems was about the sky, the other about silence. Here are the first nine lines from the two poems based on lies about the sky. From "Sky":

> At night among the stars we see
> the ever-present animals and heroes,

which preceded us. The gods
we placed there have fallen,
and the sky is thinner now
without them, lighter than
an invisible hand. It's amazing
we can touch it, that it's as close
as it is far.

And from "The Other Side of the Sky":

When God was waiting
to be invented, the sky
was thinner. You
could have touched it,
then turned away
without the fear of being seen,
gone back
to your father's house
where everything was quiet.

In the chapbook we didn't identify whose poem was
whose. Reading them now I'm not sure. I like not being
sure.

This was "play" and we kept it that way. I want to give
one example of a loopy assignment triggering a more
consequential poem. I know some of my assignments pro-
voked poems from Stephen, but he's too good at covering
his tracks. I have to settle for one of his assignments and
one of my poems. This is from a list of six assignments he
gave me in the summer of 2010 while we were at Yaddo.
One assignment from that list mandated the inclusion of

Muddy Waters, Aretha Franklin, and Glenn Campbell, and had to begin "In the secret, dark corridors of Cedar Rapids," which, except for the specificity of Cedar Rapids, already sounded like a line of mine, and not a very good one (which Stephen probably knew).

The assignment I finally completed was the most outrageously complicated of any of Stephen's assignments (so far), and so intricate that I finally saw the only way I could respond to it was to steal it and turn it into the poem it already almost was.

First, the assignment: "Write a poem from the viewpoint of someone who used to be in love with an imaginary woman. Your speaker is only sure that he wishes to have power, wishes to control the terms of his life. His stutter, or other handicap, keeps getting in the way. You'll need an adjective for bedroom, and an adjective that makes the forest he keeps returning to seem run-down, a kind of bad neighborhood. Then an adjective before 'path,' which changes the meaning of it. The imaginary woman should appear at some point, throwing everything into question. Think of your poem as an examination of an obsession, and perhaps the sadness of being cured of it."

My poem is called "A Difficult Assignment," and appropriately it was published in an issue of the *Cortland Review* devoted to Stephen's work. I see now that I failed at the end to find the adjective that would change the meaning of "path." In fact I never looked for it. The poem didn't seem to need it. Perhaps the adjective's absence is a secret sign of my resistance to the assignment's authority. Or perhaps it's something only Stephen and I—and now you—know is missing.

A Difficult Assignment

(for and after Stephen Dunn)

You'll need an adjective for bedroom,
another that makes the forest you keep returning to

seem run-down, a kind of bad neighborhood.
Then an adjective before "path," which changes

the meaning of it, as if you weren't going to end up
where you planned. Or the opposite—

you can't help where you're going. And where
would that be? It's up to you, but remember,

in all of this you should be alone
although at some point a beautiful woman

must appear, throwing everything into question.
That's when the false note rings true.

Maybe she has something to say about Cedar Rapids
or Muddy Waters. She's imaginary,

she can say anything you want. Yes,
how much she desires you is one kind of beginning,

but another might involve looking carefully
at the flowers at the edge of the forest, asking her

their names, then suggesting you don't care
where the path leads if that's where she wants to go.

What I've been describing—and there's much more, since we've been doing this for more than thirty years—results in making poems easier to begin and harder to finish. We keep each other on track, changing the meaning of "path" as we go.

In the best Dunn poems, revision—rethinking—is a central concern; perceptions are deceptive, and accessibility is a tactic, casually inviting the reader into a complicated, provocative, and often disturbing moral landscape.

And somewhere a philosopher is erasing
"time's empty passing" because he's seen
a woman in a ravishing dress.
In a different hour he'll put it back.

About these lines of Stephen's maybe I once said, Is "empty" really the best word? Or: What about another adjective—"red," perhaps—before "dress"? Maybe I said, Why are there always ravishing women in your poems? Maybe I just said, Yes, you got it.

These four lines are the end of the title poem of Stephen's collection, *Different Hours*. A lesser poet would have used the moment to choose sides, suggesting the triumph of the physical world over abstract thinking. But Stephen knows better. What engages him is the continuing tension between beauty and circumstance, between the truth of the world and the truth of what we want it to be. At one moment we are overwhelmed; and then we think differently. We change our minds, we revise our lives. The revisions of thought—and the subsequent transformations of the imagination—are Stephen's central subjects, and his poems are enactments of those concerns. The reader is not told what to think; the reader is seduced into the process of thinking, as if by a good friend who believes deeply in the value of disagreement.

Then a beautiful woman in a ravishing red dress walks past. You're sitting in a sidewalk café drinking coffee. Once she might have seen you, turned, maybe smiled. Now she continues down the street into her own particular future. The sky clouds over. A little wind flaps the striped umbrella above your table. Maybe it will rain, maybe not. Time passes like this—empty *and* ravishing. You're desolate, then amazed.

Forgetting: On "At Evening"

One of the problems of writing an elegy is that it needs to discover a subject beyond—or in addition to—grief. When the poet sits down to write, grief is an occasion for thought. Yet we know well that sorrow and loss can be so all-consuming as to block other kinds of feeling, other ways of thinking. This is why Wordsworth's famous formulation that poetry arises from "emotions recollected in tranquility" is useful. We need distance to figure out what we can do with what we have felt. We need tranquility to generate the turmoil of thought.

My mother, Marjorie Young Raab, died on March 20, 1978, which was also my daughter's first birthday. I knew at the time that was a fact I'd never want to use. How could a poem survive such an overpowering irony? And yet, writing that sentence now, more than thirty years later, it seems more like a challenge, a very difficult assignment. If I were to try to write that poem I imagine its initial subject would have to be what to make of such an irony. And in the process I'd have to be willing to allow my mother to become merely incidental, a way to get to materials I couldn't know until I got there.

After my mother's death, I wrote a number of poems about her, and some of them I ended up keeping. The ones that failed were assertions rather than considerations of how I was feeling. Probably the best of those I saved is "At Evening," which was composed years later. Its occasion consists of mostly tranquil moments of recollection. Its subject is forgetting.

My mother died suddenly of a heart attack. She was sixty-four. The shock of her death made me feel that something essential had been taken away from the world. Her death—or more precisely, her absence—seemed to affect everything I experienced, at least for a while. Remembering, for our family, was the essential, and sharable, component of mourning. But slowly we all started remembering less and less. We had to. This is where grief leads—back to the world that now continues without the person we loved. So a different kind of loss is created, not of the person herself, but of the act of remembering her. We forget to remember, and later, even more painfully, we find we cannot summon up the tone of her voice, the color of her eyes, the way she would laugh or smile.

I've never gone back to visit my mother's grave, but I can understand why people do this. It must create a ritual that allows remembering to be contained and located, or that substitutes for the inability to remember. Consequently, the inevitable dailiness of forgetting becomes more natural, releasing us, at least in part, from guilt. In Robert Frost's great poem, "Home Burial," the husband wants to move beyond his child's death, though he doesn't have the skill to describe his emotions, and so he seems unfeeling to his wife, who possesses a keener sense of language, but who has wedded herself to sorrow. "I won't have grief so / If I can change it," she cries out toward the end of the poem. But she cannot change it, only prolong it, freezing herself to the moment of gazing at the grave.

Frost's genius is to keep a rigorous balance between these two people, and so implicate the reader in their desperate struggle. We may be tempted to choose sides to gain a hold on what "Home Burial" has to say about grief and grieving, or what we may want it to say. But Frost has designed his poem to frustrate any conclusion that does not account for complexities of feeling. After all, it's the wife who sees how grief can work to allow men and women to make "the best of their way back to life / And living people, and things they understand." Yet she rejects this: "But the world's evil." If the husband can't say how he feels, she can't understand the truth of what she's said. She doesn't know that what she knows could heal her, but she's certain her husband cannot possibly feel what he should be feeling. Her last words to him are, "How can I make you—" . . . Presumably, the word she doesn't say is "understand." We can see this, or suppose it. But her husband does not, or cannot. The end of the poem locks them both into incomplete sentences.

I don't know what I would experience if I returned to my mother's grave. Nothing, I imagine, except the pressure to feel something I wasn't feeling. It would be stagy, like a shot in a film you know is set up to make a point. The end of "At Evening" moves toward a moment that includes me without thinking. As the writer I've arranged it, of course, but as the speaker I'm taken by surprise. I see the fireflies and stars as "flickering emblems," and out of this intersection of the real and the symbolic a tranquility emerges "in which remembering might not be an obligation." It's like a moment in which a poem might be made. This allows me to speak to my mother directly: "You would know what I mean." Yet the final line—"You would have known what I mean"—is a correction, a quiet admission of the obdurate fact of the past, as well as an assertion that the intimacy suggested by the previous sentence can be both an illusion and a necessary invention.

At Evening

(for my mother)

At first everything reminded us of you.
We couldn't help remembering, wanting
to talk about it together. We understood
this was the way grief works
to return us to ourselves—no discoveries
or revelations, just the old stories
full of incident and detail.

Then your death grew quieter,
a suspicion the world would always seem
vaguely wrong, as when turning a corner
we recognize someone who isn't there.
Or when a storm, pushed up for hours
against the mountains, swerves off
and only the ordinary afternoon remains.

Six years now: marking the time
season by season. So we say without thinking
of the first warm days of spring: "Like last year."
And when we decorate the tree: "Last Christmas . . . "
Left out, you move farther away,
no longer even the image of yourself
but an idea of absence, sad and abstract.

Around the house you never saw us living in
the ragged music of the crows does not
remind me of what you might have said.
It's summer, the heavy peonies shredding
out onto the grass. And at evening
the light is dense and delicate,
the mountains arranged in a purity of blue
tier after tier. So that a sense

of comfort begins to include me,
without acknowledgment. A last crow
clatters back into the pines.
One by one: fireflies, stars.
So many flickering emblems—and this stillness
in which remembering might not be an obligation.
You would know what I mean,
you would have known what I mean.

First Love: On Lewis Carroll's "Jabberwocky"

One sure sign of a real poem is our desire to hear it again. I recall my mother reading and re-reading "Jabberwocky" to me at bedtime—the pure pleasure of language being playful, especially those "slithy toves," how they'd "gyre and gimble in the wabe," and how I'd imagine myself as my mother's "beamish boy," returning home after slaying the fantastic beast.

"Poetry," Gertrude Stein said, "is really loving the name of anything." "Jabberwocky" is a poem about loving the names of things, of things we do not know beyond their names—"borogroves," "mome raths"—but find ourselves compelled to imagine.

"It seems very pretty," Alice remarks after reading the poem, "but it's *rather* hard to understand!" And in a sly parenthetical observation, Carroll notes that Alice "didn't like to confess, even to herself, that she couldn't make it out at all." "Somehow," Alice continues, "it seems to fill my head with ideas—only I don't exactly know what they are!"

Perhaps poetry exists most powerfully in the moment of unrealized possibility—imminence at the edge of meaning. It's alluring to want to remain there, as if certainty could be only reductive, and the sensible merely sensible, colorless, and disappointing. But Alice, that reasonable child, wants to know. So, chapters later, when she encounters Humpty-Dumpty, whom she recognizes as being "very clever at explaining words," Alice asks for the meaning of the poem.

As a child, I don't remember considering Humpty-Dumpty's brilliant close analysis of the first stanza of "Jabberwocky." Reading it now, I find it both wonderful and wrong, as of course it should be, spoken by a critic who claims he can "explain all the poems that ever were invented—and a good many that haven't been invented just yet." Humpty-Dumpty tells Alice that a "borogrove" is "a thin shabby-looking bird with its feathers sticking out all round—something like a live mop." But I'm sure I imagined some mysterious and slightly dangerous part of a forest, some kind of a grove, a place one might disappear into, deceptive because it was "mimsy," ominous because of those "mome raths" nearby.

Certainly Humpy-Dumpty goes out on a limb when he claims that a "rath" is "a sort of green pig." But I love that certainty, and also the fact that he admits he's not sure about "mome," adding, "I think it's short for 'from home'—meaning that they'd lost their way, you know." Isn't that what happens with the first poems we encounter? We lose our way, but we make it home in the end. "Hard stuff," Humpty-Dumpty says. And then we fall asleep.

'Twas brillig, and the slithy toves
   Did gyre and gimble in the wabe:
All mimsy were the borogoves,
   And the mome raths outgrabe.

"Beware the Jabberwock, my son!
   The jaws that bite, the claws that catch!
Beware the Jubjub bird, and shun
   The frumious Bandersnatch!"

He took his vorpal sword in hand:
    Long time the manxome foe he sought—
So rested he by the Tumtum tree,
    And stood awhile in thought.

And, as in uffish thought he stood,
    The Jabberwock, with eyes of flame,
Came whiffling through the tulgey wood,
    And burbled as it came!

One, two! One, two! And through and through
    The vorpal blade went snicker-snack!
He left it dead, and with its head
    He went galumphing back.

"And, has thou slain the Jabberwock?
    Come to my arms, my beamish boy!
O frabjous day! Callooh! Callay!"
    He chortled in his joy.

'Twas brillig, and the slithy toves
    Did gyre and gimble in the wabe;
All mimsy were the borogoves,
    And the mome raths outgrabe.

Why Don't We Say What We Mean? On Robert Frost's "Mending Wall"

Robert Frost once said that "Mending Wall" was a poem that was spoiled by being applied. What did he mean by "applied"? Any poem is damaged by being misunderstood, which is a risk all poems run. What Frost objects to is a reduction and distortion of the poem through practical use. When President Kennedy inspected the Berlin Wall he quoted the poem's first line: "Something there is that doesn't love a wall." His audience knew what he meant and how the quotation applied. And on the other side of that particular wall, we can find another example of how the poem has been used. Returning from a visit to Russia late in his life, Frost said, "The Russians reprinted 'Mending Wall' over there, and left that first line off." He added wryly, "I don't see how they got the poem started." What the Russians needed, and so took, was the poem's other detachable statement: "Good fences make good neighbors." They applied what they wanted. "I could've done better for them, probably," Frost said, "for the generality, by saying: 'Something there is that doesn't love a wall, / Something there is that does.'" "Why didn't I say that?" Frost asked rhetorically. "I didn't mean that. I meant to leave that until later in the poem. I left it there."

"Mending Wall" famously contains these two apparently conflicting statements. One begins the poem, the other ends it, and both are repeated twice. Which are we supposed to believe? What does Frost mean? "The secret of what it means I keep," he said. Of course he was being cagey, but not without reason.

At a reading given at the Library of Congress in 1962, Frost told this anecdote:

> In England, two or three years ago, Graham Greene said to me, "The most difficult thing I find in recent literature is your having said that good fences make good neighbors."
>
> And I said, "I wish you knew more about it, without my helping you."
>
> We laughed, and I left it that way.

Why doesn't Frost want to say what he meant? When asked, he'd reply, "What do you want me to do, say it again in different and less good words?"

"You get more credit for thinking," Frost wrote in a letter, "if you restate formulae or cite cases that fall in easily under formulae, but all the fun is outside: saying things that suggest formulae that won't formulate—that almost but don't quite formulate." A formula is the easy answer that turns out to be, though right or wrong in general, certainly inadequate in particular. A formula, like a paraphrase of the poem itself, is made of those "less good words" the poet has tried to resist.

"Mending Wall" seems to present us with a problem, and appears to urge us to choose sides. I suspect most readers are eager to ally themselves with the speaker, to consider the neighbor dim-witted, block-headed, and generally dull. Such a reading is nicely represented by the following passage from a booklet on Frost put out by Monarch Notes:

By the end of the poem [the wall] has become a symbol, and the two farmers have turned into allegorical figures representing opposing views of freedom and confinement, reason and rigidity of mind, tolerance and violence, civilization and savagery . . . There is no mistaking the poet's meaning, or his attitude toward what the wall represents . . . it stands for . . . the barrier between human contact and understanding. It is erected by all that is primitive, fearful, irrational and hostile [in the neighbor]. It is opposed by a higher "something" that Frost recognizes in himself . . . the desire not to be alone, walled in, but to be one with the rest of the world.

There is no mistaking what the authors of the Monarch Notes want to believe, and on which side of the wall they stand. And of course it's comforting to believe that the poem suggests we could be "one with the rest of the world." But is that what the poem actually says? "Mending Wall" opens with a riddle: "Something there is . . . " And a riddle, after all, is a series of hints calculated to make us imagine and then name its hidden subject. The poem doesn't begin, "I hate walls." Or even, "Something dislikes a wall." Its first gesture is one of elaborate and playful concealment, a calculated withholding of meaning. Notice also that it is the speaker himself who repairs the wall after the hunters have broken it. And it is the speaker each year who notifies his neighbor when the time has come to meet and mend the wall. Then can we safely claim that the speaker views the wall simply as a barrier between human contact and understanding?

Speaker and neighbor work together and equally. Although the job is tedious and hard, the speaker considers it "just another kind of outdoor game / One on a side." He acknowledges that his whimsical spell—"Stay where you are until our backs are turned!"—is useless, and that the result is impermanent and perhaps less important than something else. For all practical purposes this particular wall is not needed. But the project of mending it has taken on significance: "Spring is the mischief in me, and I wonder / If I could put a notion in his head . . ."

The speaker's mischievous impulse is to plant an idea. He does not say that he wants to change his neighbor's mind, to make him believe what he himself believes. He wants to nudge the neighbor's imagination, just as a teacher might wish to challenge a student. So he asks questions: "*Why* do they make good neighbors? Isn't it / Where there are cows? But here there are no cows." But the neighbor is unwilling to play this game of teacher and student. He won't answer the questions, or consider the riddle. The speaker could suggest "Elves" but "it's not elves exactly," and of course it's not elves at all. The speaker's frustration is beginning to get the better of him. He wants to be fanciful—he wants to talk—and his neighbor does not. More importantly, and again like a good teacher, "I'd rather / He said it for himself."

"I wish you knew more about it," Frost says he told Graham Greene, "without my helping you." This is the poem's essential challenge, which the neighbor will not accept. But the challenge is ours as well—our work, our play. The relationship between speaker and neighbor is like the relationship between poem and reader, another kind of game, one on a side.

This is a relationship between poem and reader, not poet and reader. Frost, I want to believe, is not the speaker *exactly*. He is behind the whole poem, rather than narrowly inside it. We need to be at least a little skeptical of the speaker. At the end, because the neighbor won't play his game, the speaker imagines him as "an old-stone savage," a harsh judgment to apply even to the most recalcitrant student. Because the neighbor will only repeat what he remembers his father having said, he seems to "move in darkness . . . Not of woods only and the shade of trees." But of what else? We should say it for ourselves. Ignorance? Confinement, violence, and savagery, as the Monarch authors have it? Not exactly. It's his refusal to be playful and imaginative that irks the speaker, and his unwillingness to consider work as anything more than a job to be accomplished. The speaker, after all, does not ask the neighbor to give up his father's notion. He wants him to "go behind" it. If, as I want to suggest, the poem is about education, this distinction is important. The poem does not merely advocate one position over another. It asks neither for advocacy nor for application, but for investigation. It is not a statement but a performance.

Who, finally, is right about the wall? The poem does not answer that question exactly, swerving off into deeper and more interesting territory. It *uses* that problem to engage us and demand that we think, which is the poem's pleasure, and its strategy. Sometimes good fences do indeed make good neighbors, and we might recall that the phrase "mending fences" means to restore communication and neighborliness. Equally true is the notion that something doesn't love a wall. The riddle isn't a difficult one.

We know that natural forces disturb those boulders, that the frozen groundswell is frost. But not, for all the play of the pun, "Robert Frost." "All the fun's in how you say a thing," says a character in another Frost poem. But fun can be serious, just as work can be turned into play.

> I let my neighbor know beyond the hill;
> And on a day we meet to walk the line
> And set the wall between us once again.
> We keep the wall between us as we go.

The repetition of *between* should give us pause and remind us of its two equally common meanings: *between* as separation, as in "something's come between us," and *between* as what might be shared and held in common, as in "a secret between two people" or "a bond between friends." The wall divides but it also connects, if you look at it that way. All the meaning is in how you look at it—how the poem encourages you to think about it.

Frost once wrote about his experience as a teacher, "I was determined to have it out with my youngers and betters as to what thinking really was. We reached an agreement that most of what they had regarded as thinking, their own and other peoples', was nothing but voting—taking sides on an issue they had nothing to do with laying down." "Mending Wall" is a poem that lures the unwary reader into believing that thinking is merely voting, choosing sides, taking out of the poem what most fits our own preconceived ideas. It adopts this tactic because its ultimate purpose is to challenge us to "go behind" what we might find initially appealing in the formulas that lie on the surface. "We ask people to think," Frost says, "and we don't show them what thinking is." "Mending Wall" is less a poem about what to think than it is a poem about what thinking is, and where it might lead.

In his essay "Education by Poetry," Frost writes,

> Poetry provides the one permissible way of saying one thing and meaning another. People say, 'Why don't you say what you mean?' We never do that, do we, being all of us too much poets. We like to talk in parables and in hints and in indirections— whether from diffidence or some other instinct.

Perhaps we are, all of us, so much poets, or might be, but Frost, who certainly was, doesn't really answer his question. Surely diffidence is not the reason why writers are drawn to the indirections of figurative language. What might that "other instinct" be? One answer is the instinct of the teacher who speaks in hints, in questions, and in challenges, who refrains from saying what he or she means in the hopes that the students will discover it for themselves. Similarly, the apparent meaning of a poem remains merely a formula unless the reader has understood how the poem came to articulate and embody that meaning. The speaker of "Mending Wall" fails in his attempt to become a successful poet/teacher. Each year, it seems, he fails at the same task. Frost's poem depends upon and survives this failure, as long as we do not demand that it say what it means.

Mending Wall

Something there is that doesn't love a wall,
That sends the frozen-ground-swell under it,
And spills the upper boulders in the sun;
And makes gaps even two can pass abreast.
The work of hunters is another thing:
I have come after them and made repair
Where they have left not one stone on a stone,
But they would have the rabbit out of hiding,
To please the yelping dogs. The gaps I mean,
No one has seen them made or heard them made,
But at spring mending-time we find them there.
I let my neighbor know beyond the hill;
And on a day we meet to walk the line
And set the wall between us once again.
We keep the wall between us as we go.
To each the boulders that have fallen to each.
And some are loaves and some so nearly balls
We have to use a spell to make them balance:
'Stay where you are until our backs are turned!'
We wear our fingers rough with handling them.
Oh, just another kind of out-door game,
One on a side. It comes to little more:
There where it is we do not need the wall:
He is all pine and I am apple orchard.
My apple trees will never get across
And eat the cones under his pines, I tell him.
He only says, 'Good fences make good neighbors.'
Spring is the mischief in me, and I wonder
If I could put a notion in his head:

'*Why* do they make good neighbors? Isn't it
Where there are cows? But here there are no cows.
Before I built a wall I'd ask to know
What I was walling in or walling out,
And to whom I was like to give offense.
Something there is that doesn't love a wall,
That wants it down.' I could say 'Elves' to him,
But it's not elves exactly, and I'd rather
He said it for himself. I see him there
Bringing a stone grasped firmly by the top
In each hand, like an old-stone savage armed.
He moves in darkness as it seems to me,
Not of woods only and the shade of trees.
He will not go behind his father's saying,
And he likes having thought of it so well
He says again, 'Good fences make good neighbors.'

Thinking Out Loud: On Wisława Szymborska

One of the ways a poem can be eloquent is by pretending to have nothing to do with eloquence. This strategy has many dangers. If we catch the writer cultivating modesty, or putting on airs while pretending to do the opposite, the poem's plainness will appear calculated for effect. Of course we know that all good art has been calculated for effect. Nevertheless, the directness of certain poems can seem wholly natural, as if the poet desired only to speak in the clearest possible way, saying just what needs to be said.

Wisława Szymborska's poems feel like this, like unpremeditated thought, which is, at the same time, thinking of such clarity that its complications continually surprise us. The poems are accessible, the words apparently simple. They say what we almost thought of saying: "After every war / someone has to tidy up. / Things won't pick / themselves up, after all." Yes, that's true. And so this poem continues, off-handedly accumulating its devastating perceptions, as if a resigned but overburdened parent were speaking—a mother, no doubt. Can't you remember to pick your things up and put them away? she complains. But the children never remember. And knowing how easily someone could trip over that ball or that truck, the mother sighs and returns those toys to their places. So, at night, the women go out onto the field of battle to retrieve the bodies.

"In the language of poetry," Szymborska says in her Nobel lecture, "where every word is weighed, nothing is usual or normal." And yet the illusion is of a normality, however frightening, and the sign of this is the fraught tension between the word "war" and the phrase "tidy up." Something feels askew here. And indeed something is, which the language reveals by pretending to use the wrong words for the occasion. So after every war someone "has to shove / the rubble to the roadsides / so the carts loaded with corpses / can get by." This is the way it goes, and the horror of the moment lies in the absence of horror in the language. This is what people have allowed the everyday to become.

And yet: "Someone, broom in hand, / still remembers how it was. / Someone else listens, nodding / his unshattered head." The greatest surprise in these lines is "unshattered," a word that gives what it takes away, or perhaps takes away what it gives. At first we see the shattered head of the victim, then we realize that the word actually means the opposite of what we couldn't help but visualize. The person who might have been destroyed is whole, his head undamaged. The one who is remembering, broom in hand, could be the poet, just as I, as the reader, could be the one nodding his head. But we aren't permitted to linger in this reflective moment, as if such communion were a kind of victory of the intelligence. At the end of the poem, called "The End and the Beginning," remembering is lost:

> Those who knew
> what this was all about
> must make way for those
> who know little.
> And less than that.
> And at last nothing less
> than nothing.

The movement is from little to less to nothing, but no—it's even worse, it's "nothing less than nothing." This is not exactly nothing minus nothing, which could still be *something*, small and fragile as it might be. But if nothing follows less than a little, how can there be less than nothing? Here—rather than the weighed language of "tidy" or "unshattered"—it's Symborska's phrasing that disturbs and disorients us. On the one hand, we seem to be presented with a kind of metaphysical problem. On the other, we're being told simply that everything is worse than we can imagine.

But Syzborska now is not speaking of the devastation of battle but of the losses of memory. And these, sadly, are inevitable. Those who knew "must make way" for those who don't. But is this sad, or just natural? If the world were too devastating, who could go on, who would even want to try to put the pieces back together? At the end of the poem someone—a boy I've imagined—lies in the expanse of a field that conceals the past. The grass "covers up / the causes and effects," and this survivor, who does not think of himself as a survivor, lazily gazes up at the sky with a cornstalk in his teeth. Can we blame him for what he doesn't know? He's just "gawking at the clouds," like a kid.

In "Nervousness," one of her short prose pieces, Szymborska recalls a group reading in Krakow in 1945, the first such occasion after the end of the war. Many participated, and "not everyone read well," though Szymborska admits her knowledge of poetry then "equaled zero." She was just listening; her first book wouldn't appear for another twelve years. "At a certain moment," she writes, "they announced someone named Miłosz. He read calmly, without histrionics. As if he were simply thinking out loud and inviting us to join him. 'There you go,' I told myself, 'that's real poetry, there's a real poet.'"

Craft disappears into content. That's the illusion. Some people listen, and hear themselves listening, as if their attentiveness were part of the thinking of the poem itself, which then includes them. "Poetry— / but what is poetry anyway?" Szymborska asks in "Some People Like Poetry":

> More than one rickety answer
> has tumbled since that question first was raised.
> But I just keep on not knowing, and I cling to that
> like a redemptive handrail.

On the one hand, the rickety answers. On the other, the redemptive handrail—which is *not knowing*. How easy it is to fall if one is too certain. Isn't certainty what shatters the heads, what strews the field with bodies? Not just that, of course. "I prefer," she writes in "Possibilities," "keeping in mind even the possibility that existence has its own reason for being." And so, in a typical move, she catches us thinking a little less expansively than she has been thinking, but she takes us along. And poetry—where does that fit in? "I prefer the absurdity of writing poems / to the absurdity of not writing poems." Yes, I tell myself. That's what I want to hold on to.

3

■

A Clock Called the Wind: René Magritte and the Mysteries of Metaphor

"To equate my painting with symbolism," René Magritte writes, "conscious or unconscious, is to ignore its true nature." Magritte would have admitted that his pictures *use* symbols. What he wants to resist is the translation of the suggestiveness of the image into the inflexibility of the symbol. Magritte continues:

> People who look for symbolic meanings fail to grasp the inherent poetry and mystery of the image. No doubt they sense this mystery, but they wish to get rid of it. They are afraid. By asking "what does this mean?" they express a wish that everything be understandable. But if one does not reject the mystery, one has quite a different response. One asks other things.

What other things? Magritte doesn't say, his business being to make things, not to explain them; to provoke, not to reassure. He knows that people prefer to remain comfortable and unafraid. They turn to meaning for security. Symbolism can provide that, and in its crudest form a symbol is a representation *of* something—something understandable. An image can deliver the symbolic as efficiently as it can produce its own name. But the name—the valise which is called a valise, the clock which is called a clock—is merely what's been attached to an object so we can identify it and therefore use it, carry things around in it, tell the time. Other names will fit as easily, as Magritte's

1936 painting *The Key of Dreams* suggests. This picture is divided into four equal parts, each containing a single image on a dark background with a caption. The images have the flat realism of a child's first reading book, a thing paired with the name by which it is known. So a valise is called "the valise," but to the left of it a pitcher is called "the bird." Above the pitcher a horse is labeled "the door," and to the right of the horse is a clock called "the wind."

Magritte no doubt knew the risk of his work, how easily its "true nature" could be avoided or dismissed. Taken for granted, anything loses its sense of presence, fading from sight while at the same time remaining visible. But freed from the context of the familiar, the thing reasserts itself. The tortoise-shell comb in *Personal Values* (1952), by appearing huge in its ordinary room, or ordinary in its miniature room, reclaims its exact shape, rescues itself from over-familiarity. In addition to the comb (which leans upright on a bed against the wall) there are four other objects: a match, a glass, an oval cake of soap, and a shaving brush. The walls of the room are covered with puffy white clouds in a blue sky. Is this wallpaper? Or the sky itself?

Thus "the inherent poetry and mystery of the image" become available. A nervous viewer "no doubt" senses this mystery, and may well have been made uncomfortable by it. For example, Alexandre Iolas, Magritte's dealer, wrote to him to say that *Personal Values* depressed him, deranged him, and made him sick. It is impossible, alas, to imagine such a response today. Magritte wrote back to Iolas saying, "A really vibrant painting has to make the onlooker sick . . . "

Why? Because mystery creates at least discomfort. And

that is because mystery resists translation into meaning, which is not to say that mystery is meaningless, but that it actively *resists* becoming something other than itself. When the detective solves the case, that mystery is over and we are left with a world of reasonable explanations. Any aura of the uncanny or the impossible has been dispelled. Strangeness has become fact.

"What does it mean?" is one of the central questions that mystery, at its peril, provokes, just as the detective story asks, "Who did it?" Or "Why?" or "What happens next?" In Magritte's *The Threatened Assassin* of 1927 (also sometimes known in English as *The Murderer Threatened*, an interesting difference), the essential elements of a detective story are present but no interpretation is possible. Or else: any interpretation is possible. Any story can be invented that might lead to this moment, strange as that story would probably have to be. But the picture is about what is missing from the picture.

The painting depicts a room. In the far wall a window reveals a scene of tall, snow-covered mountain peaks. At the bottom of the window three identical and impassive men stare into the room, as well as at the viewer. On a couch is the naked corpse of a woman. Blood drips from her mouth. A scarf or towel covers her neck suggesting, given the odd position of her neck, that her head may have been severed, then the wound hidden. To the right of the woman, a well-dressed man idly listens to a record on an old gramaphone. Beside him there is a chair, his coat lying over it, and his hat resting neatly on his coat; his suitcase sits on the floor behind it, indicating, perhaps, departure or flight, but also oddly suggesting the idea of other kinds of travel, a vacation perhaps, or a business trip. This man, unmarked by any signs of violence and with a totally impassive look on his face, is presumably the murderer, or the assassin. The word "murderer" suggests passionate violence, whereas "assassin" invites us to imagine cold calculation, perhaps in the service of someone else. (The French title is *L'assassin menacé*.)

But it's fruitless to try to ascribe emotions to any of these people since all of the men in the painting have identical faces. To either side of the entrance to this room, hidden from the murderer's sight, are two bowler-hatted men, one holding a club, the other a large net. Are these men the police, about to capture—or club to death—the murderer? Yet there's no indication that they're police. Who are the observers outside the window, and is there a fourth man, unseen because the murderer's shoulder covers that part of the window? Why has the murder been committed, and so brutally? Will the murderer escape? Why is he not hurrying away from the scene of the crime? What song is he listening to? What, for him, is the particular meaning of that song?

We see a moment from a mystery—a kind of bizarre genre scene—in which everything is unclear. If this were a still from a film, or an illustration from a story, we could expect to find out. But we don't find out, and can't hope to. Is the aim of the painting, then, to frustrate us? Yes. But what can we do with that frustration—that wanting to know—except admit that the painting is about this kind of desire, coupled with our not being able to know?

What's important is not to avoid asking, "What does it mean?" (which in any case would be impossible), but to avoid settling for that question. We may wish that everything were understandable, but we know it isn't. So if we do not reject the mystery, we ask "other things," one of which might be: Why do I need to know what it means? Or: What do I want it to mean? Or even: How can I live with what can't be understood?

"The power of thought," Magritte writes in a letter from 1959, "is demonstrated by unveiling or evoking the mystery in creatures that seem familiar to us, out of error or habit." We all know how hard it is to look freshly—or look at all—at what we're accustomed to seeing every day. That mountain, that tree, that building, which a stranger might well find arresting, we pass without noticing, since mere acknowledgment is a kind of blindness. But if the tree falls, if the building burns down, absence renders them visible. Destruction and death create for a while the achingly palpable semblance of what was lost.

Yet Magritte suggests that this "unveiling or evoking," this rescuing of presence from indifference, need not be the result of violence, but can be generated by "the power of thought." The painting is designed to provoke such energy, which might eventually reveal the things of the world. But the power of thought can be defeated by the substitution of symbolic meaning for mystery, the problem being the reflexive act of substitution even more than the limitations of the symbolic. A moment of disturbance capable of producing the engagement of thought is replaced by something comfortable and secure—unearned meaning, demystified symbolism, "facile self-assurance," which, according to Magritte, must always be countered by "appropriate mistrust."

Earlier I claimed that Magritte wishes to resist the inflexibility of a "symbol." But it might be just as accurate to say that Magritte wants to cherish that inflexibility as long as he can, to use it, to set one apparently fixed symbol or object—an apple, a rose, a key, the moon—against another, counting on the friction between the two to produce the desired effect: "poetry," to use his word, rather than "meaning." So poetry freed from the constraints of meaning becomes mystery. Which is an equation that itself sounds mysterious, in the sense of being perplexing. Which Magritte would no doubt approve of. Since what he really wants to create in his paintings is not sympathetic understanding but a kind of panic. He wants to pull the rug out from under us and then insist it was no joke.

But now we might find it useful to be a little more precise about that mysterious word, *mystery*. On the one hand, we have the theological meaning: "A religious truth known only from divine revelation; usually a doctrine of the faith involving difficulties which human reason is incapable of solving." And on the other, the secular: "A hidden or secret thing, a matter unexplained or inexplicable; something beyond human knowledge or comprehension; a riddle or enigma." (Both definitions are from the *Oxford English Dictionary*.) Of course there's a very significant difference (in the second definition) between the "unexplained" and the "inexplicable," the first being solvable, the second not. I suspect Magritte would prefer the inexplicable, but also feel an affinity for the unexplained as well. No doubt he would want both, the maximum amount of complexity with the greatest visual clarity. The issue, therefore, is not just confronting a thing—a crime, an image—which is explainable or not, but grappling with those "difficulties," which we *suspect* are insoluble. The true mystery (and poetry) lies in the grappling, in the divide between the unexplained and the inexplicable, a space that vibrates with the enigmatic, with what *might* be beyond our comprehension.

Magritte's meditations on the power of an image apply to the flat unchanging surface that is a painting. You see it all at once, propped on the easel or hung on the wall. When you turn away the aura of that image may have altered your sense of what you see next, but what you see next is everything that isn't the painting. In several of Magritte's pictures (*The Human Condition*, *Euclidean Walks*, *The Fair Captive*), a painting on an easel depicts the same landscape that continues in the "actual" world around the picture. (Sometimes a window or a door further complicates the matter.) Is the unreal (the landscape in the painting) as real as the real (the landscape outside), which of course is also unreal, being part of the actual painting? And what lies behind the painting—the extension of the landscape, or something entirely different? "More of the landscape" would be the immediate and conventional response. "A bowler-hatted man" would be a more disruptive possibility. But the answer, Magritte would no doubt say, is "nothing at all." What is suggested but cannot be seen in a painting is simply not there. And that's what we are invited to imagine, and then forced to deny, which is like the move from the unexplained to the inexplicable.

Nothing but blank canvas is the challenge—to try to see and fail to see what can't be seen, to solve a crime that can't be solved. And whether we imagine nothing or something, the world beyond the painting within the painting becomes a kind of refraction of the image, however stable or unbent it may seem, a likeness or unlikeness, a sort of metaphor—the tense relationship of similarity and its ultimate collapse.

■

"Metaphor," Aristotle asserts, "consists in giving the thing a name that belongs to something else." As its origin in the Greek word for *transfer* suggests, metaphor is a process of conveying, as well as of sharing, some quality. We are accustomed to using likenesses, consciously or unconsciously, to communicate the appearance of a place or the effect of an experience, as well as to fix meaning, so that we can go about our lives and say, with some assurance, that a particular intent will be understood: "Where is my valise?" or "Please pass that pitcher of milk." But as Magritte's *Key of Dreams* demonstrates, that process can be disrupted. If the thing is given a different, seemingly inappropriate name, suspicion is created that implicates both word and image.

The clock with its caption of "the wind" looks like a metaphor, though it may be a metaphor that doesn't work, or works only to reveal difference instead of likeness. If the phrase "the clock which is the wind," or "the clock of wind," were to appear in a poem, it might seem persuasively surreal, or perhaps merely fanciful. But how easily a sensible mind can transform the strangeness of "the clock of wind" into the numbingly ordinary "winds of time."

When a thing is too obviously like something else, the

metaphor fails to generate any visual or intellectual excitement. It only makes sense. It's the illustration we didn't need, bad pedagogy. But the farther apart two things are, the more dangerous and demanding the metaphor becomes, the more we're aware of the evocative difficulty of the act of transference, as in the always startling opening of T. S. Eliot's "Love Song of J. Alfred Prufrock":

> Let us go then, you and I,
> When the evening is spread out against the sky
> Like a patient etherised upon a table . . .

The "unveiling or evoking" that Magritte talks about when citing the "power of thought" is essentially a function of metaphor (or simile, in Eliot's lines). But instead of making strangeness familiar, Magritte's metaphors produce mystery from the apparently ordinary, just as the third line of "Prufrock" completely destroys the pallid romantic expectations of the poem's first two lines. The predictable beauty of an evening that might be like some assemblage of angels or gossamer veils is suddenly blown apart, and there, drugged and spread out between reality and dream, is Prufrock's evening, violently reconfigured.

But likeness is temporary and fragile. Part of the beauty and importance of the metaphorical *process* lies in knowing how far you can go, when the metaphor will start to fail, and therefore when you can no longer trust it.

"My love is a rose" (or maybe *like* a rose) a poet once wrote for the first time, meaning that roses, like the beloved, look beautiful and smell sweet, not that they have thorns and can puncture your skin. That's where the metaphor breaks down and fails, or where a crafty poet attempts to turn it against itself. When Gertrude Stein wrote her famous circle of "A rose is a rose is a rose is a rose . . . " she claimed the rose was red for the first time in a hundred years. (Of course poetry-roses are always red, just as violets are blue.) But Stein makes a good point, however much she may overstate her accomplishment. The surprise of the repetition, combined with the loveliness of the circle, also suggest that her metaphor is one of perfect equality. A rose can best be defined by invoking its own name. It is what it is. As simple as that.

The opposite effect—of horror—is achieved by Pablo Neruda using the same strategy in his well-known line in "I'm Explaining a Few Things": ". . . the blood of the children ran through the streets / without fuss, like children's blood." Metaphors, these lines suggest, are insufficient to the occasion—too contrived, perhaps, or too poetic. The blood is the blood. But this effect—and this kind of thinking and feeling—are achieved by the *anticipation* of a metaphorical comparison. *Like* points to what we expect, which is difference. Nothing I can invent, Neruda says, can be like this.

This strategy is reversed (or elaborated, perhaps) in Magritte's famous tease of a painting of a pipe with the words "This is not a pipe" written beneath it. The "answer" is: of course it's not an *actual* pipe; it's a painting of a pipe. But the image can take us farther. The pipe, by being denied its name, assumes the form of . . . *a pipe,* if not for the first time in a hundred years, then perhaps for a while. We look at the painting of the pipe to discover how it may not be a pipe, that is, how the inscription could be true. But it *is* a pipe; if only a representation of a pipe.

Nevertheless, the denial has made us look. Had the inscription been, "This is a pipe," we would have seen little, passed by quickly, and merely acknowledged the obvious.

■

As I was thinking of Magritte's pipe, Neruda's blood, and Stein's rose, a song called "Love Interruption" by Jack Black came on the radio. The first verse is:

> I want love to
> Roll me over slowly
> Stick a knife inside me
> And twist it all around.

The first two lines suggest a rather conventional image of tenderness, with "love"—not "my love"—personified. The third line changes the mood. And yet aren't we still in the presence of the familiar? The turn from tenderness to violence is easily read in terms of *passion*. I want to be *ravished* by love. I want to die (pun intended) by it, knifed in the heart. Think of how naturally we accept a "knife," how different it would be if we were given an icepick. Now consider an image of a knife with, perhaps, a drop of blood at its tip, and beneath it the word "Love." Easy enough to understand; easy enough to turn into a tattoo.

But Black's fourth line is more unsettling. The metaphorical knife in the heart becomes unpleasantly graphic. The "pain of love" slides into sadism. Twisting the knife "all around" evokes a violence greater than the trope behind the image. Love hurts. But this knife really hurts.

Jack Black's song continues in a similar, but often less surprising, mode, until the fourth verse, which is stranger:

> I want love to
> Change my friends to enemies
> Change my friends to enemies
> And show me how it's all my fault.

The issue is expectation, as with Stein and Neruda. We had a series of comparisons and we anticipate another, but these lines break away from the metaphorical scaffolding that had earlier supported love's transformation from sweetness to violence. Yet they still retain the personification of love, leading us in a figurative direction we'd become accustomed to, but now are not given. One of the ways a metaphor can work to surprise us is by surprising us with its absence.

■

We may initially think that by seeing one thing in terms of another we will see more clearly. But will we? Is this the aim of metaphor? It is, in part. It certainly is for the poet who compares his love to a rose rather than saying, "You look pretty and smell good." But he has failed if she responds with incredulity rather than with a keener understanding of his feelings—if she doesn't *get it*—and replies, "You mean I'm like some kind of *plant*?"

A metaphor serves to intensify a perception, but it also embodies feeling and thought. It is a *way* of seeing, and that way becomes a revelation of the sensibility of the metaphor-maker. The metaphor embodies emotions and ideas though the specificity of perception. As Ezra Pound writes, "An image is that which presents an intellectual and emotional complex in an instant of time."

Consequently, what lies behind a successful metaphor is a singularity of seeing, proving that nothing in the world is just itself. Or rather: Nothing can just be seen *as* itself. As John Berger writes, "A drawing of a tree shows not a tree but a tree being looked at." A "lonely" tree and a "mournful" wind reflect and embody a particular viewer's emotions, since wind and tree contain no value in themselves. Observation imposes feeling upon them. We can never see without the imposition of personality, and that imposition, consciously considered, finds its most powerful shape in metaphor.

"People," says Magritte, "are quite willing to use objects without looking for any specific intention in them . . . " Of course this is not exactly true. People use objects casually because they assume they know what their intentions are—a knife cuts meat, a glass holds water. *Personal Values*, for example, is a room full of intentions—objects used every day, like the comb, the match, the bed—but whose presences are excitingly called into question when placed in a tiny doll's house of a room so they *appear* gigantic, or in a normal room where they have somehow *grown* gigantic. Insofar as they appear to us freshly through these adjustments of size, they become metaphors of themselves.

"But when people look at paintings," Magritte continues, "they can't find any use for them. So they hunt around for a meaning to get themselves out of the quandary . . . they want something secure to hang on to . . . "

Meaning slides into use. Once you know what something means you know how useful it might be. Use then slides into value. How ironic that Magritte's paintings are useful now because they are valuable, and being valuable and well known, they are too easy to see. The shock wears off. The viewer's "panic" becomes complacency. It had to happen. Pictures, like metaphors, wear themselves out through over-use or mere familiarity. This is what Magritte always knew.

As he said, he desired to create an image "that resists any explication and that simultaneously resists indifference," thus evoking that essential aura of mystery. One way of resisting indifference is to coax the viewer into believing that explication is possible, and then go about preventing it, while at the same time maintaining the beauty and seductiveness of the image. In this way indifference—or *not seeing*—is defeated. Finally, we cannot ever solve the crime, but as long as we keep trying, our failure is Magritte's achievement.

Remarks as Literature: *The Autobiography of Alice B. Toklas* by Gertrude Stein

Like a good detective story, the end of *The Autobiography of Alice B. Toklas* reveals one final secret:

> About six weeks ago Gertrude Stein said, it does not look to me as if you were ever going to write that autobiography. You know what I am going to do. I am going to write it for you. I am going to write it as simply as Defoe did the autobiography of Robinson Crusoe. And she has and this is it.

Of course the secret has always been there in the title. But is this engaging sleight-of-hand only a trick, a joke, a charming pretense? We all know that the best detective stories are concerned with more than the solution of the crime. Where does Gertrude Stein's "solution" lead us? Why has she chosen to disguise herself in the voice of her companion, Alice B. Toklas?

Twice in the *Autobiography* Stein recalls her chiding of Hemingway. "Hemingway," she had said, "remarks are not literature." Yet the *Autobiography* looks curiously like a series of remarks: remarks about friends, the fading of friendships, about painters and their work and their wives, good exhibitions, good dinners, good conversation; remarks about the war, about soldiers, about driving a Ford, about art, about literature; remarks about the fact that remarks are not literature. We could say that the *Autobiography* takes the remark as one of its tactics, even one of its disguises, since it has assumed through its voice the disguise of the autobiography. But can remarks become literature?

Published in 1933, the *Autobiography* is widely considered Gertrude Stein's most likable, most accessible book—simply a story of "how two americans happened to be in the heart of an art movement of which the outside world at that time knew nothing." At first this book seems altogether different from her earlier—and later—"difficult" work, her concern with what she called "the value of the individual word." Yet the *Autobiography*'s apparent simplicity may also be a kind of mask. "I like a thing simple," she said, "but it must be simple through complication." And perhaps her more enigmatic writing—for instance, *Tender Buttons* (1914)—may not be as forbidding as the reader initially suspects. "Complicate your life as much as you please," William James had told her, "it has got to simplify." Literature also might achieve clarity through complication.

The *Autobiography* made Gertrude Stein famous, but fragments from other writings—her famous sentence, "A rose is a rose is a rose is a rose," for example, or her remark about Oakland, "There is no there there"—made her notorious. When she visited America on a lecture tour, reporters were surprised to find that she spoke plain English and they could understand what she had to say. Why don't you write the way you talk? she was asked. To which she replied: Why don't you read the way I write?

What seems confused and obscure, she maintained, might actually be clear if one could only hear it the way it was written. But readers too often assume they know how a work of literature should be read—just as everything has always been read: novel, cookbook, poem, billboard. If a book seems impenetrable, some special knowledge must be required. The book is perceived as a complicated puzzle. Keys must be found before it can be unlocked, deciphered, and decoded, then (often) reduced to the level of billboard and newspaper: the message, the news, the *meaning* comfortable, reassuring, and understandable at last.

"I never was interested in cross word puzzles or any kind of puzzles," Stein writes in her book *Everybody's Autobiography*, "but I do like detective stories. I never try to guess who has done the crime and if I did I would be sure to guess wrong but I like somebody being dead and how it moves along." How it moves along might be more than the pleasures of the surface. It might be more significant than what the book seems to be about. How it moves might be what it means.

■

"Other people's words are quite different from one's own . . . "This, Gertrude Stein claims, was one of the discoveries she made when, as a joke (as well as a conscious attempt to write a popular book), she began the autobiography that Alice seemed unlikely to ever get around to writing. And the way it moved, the way Alice's voice carried it along, would give the book the shape and control it needed to become more than a stunt or a tour de force. But there were other reasons for making Alice the speaker. There was, Stein declared, the problem of time.

In 1946 she spoke of the making of the *Autobiography*

in an interview with Robert Bartlett Haas: "You have as a person writing, and all the really great narration has it, you have to denude yourself of time so that writing time does not exist. If time exists your writing is ephemeral. You can have a historical time but for you the time does not exist and if you are writing about the present the time element must cease to exist . . . There should not be a sense of time but an existence suspended in time."

The problem of the *Autobiography* was the invention of a real historical past that would, nevertheless, subvert the pressures of "the time element." Otherwise she was sure the work would not hold up, like a painting that disappeared into the wall until she could no longer see it. Identity and memory (not just incident and description) had to become the *materials* of the composition. "If you remember while you are writing it will seem clear at the time to any one but the clarity will go out of it . . . " For Stein art had to be an expression of "the complete actual present." To write and to remember at the same moment was simply impossible. Her own past would have to be fashioned into an invented but not imaginary present. "Because if you remember yourself while you are you you are not for purposes of creating you." Therefore the artist must have no identity for the purpose of constructing the identity of the work.

Gertrude Stein could not write her own autobiography, but someone else could. Through that narration and the precise composition of that voice, the past might be redeemed and the life of memory re-created within the "actual moment" of the speaking voice of Alice B. Toklas. Therefore Gertrude Stein would write Alice's autobiography at the same moment that Alice, pretending to write her own autobiography, wrote Gertrude's biography, which is, in fact, Gertrude Stein's autobiography.

An autobiography was not unlike a mystery story in which the detective was also the victim. Just as the past was dead, so the victim also had been murdered before the story had begun. And this "victim" could hardly preside over the investigation of her own murder.

■

Early in the twentieth century, when Gertrude Stein was investigating "the value of the individual word," the first Cubist experiments were also under way. Of these paintings she wrote: "Picasso in his early cubist pictures used printed letters as did Juan Gris to force the painted surface to measure up to something rigid, and the rigid thing was the printed letter." The *Autobiography* also uses this tactic. The invented voice of Gertrude-as-Alice would function as "something rigid" and would force the past to assume a literary shape. The painted surface would be the presence and life of Gertrude Stein.

In Picasso's *Architect's Table* of 1912, a picture once owned by Stein, we see the letters that become MA JOLIE, the curves that could represent a cup on a saucer, the curl that might be part of a violin, the tilted words toward the bottom that say "Gertrude Stein." But this is not the illusion of a table, one that could be covered by a cloth and set against a wall beneath a window. The picture is the table. Content, in other words, is an excuse for art.

Long after the publication of the *Autobiography* we

have become more accustomed to, though perhaps no less comfortable with, the thought that a work of art might finally be a medium leading us to a discovery of itself *as* itself, of a shape that may or may not be primarily—or even at all—reflective of those aspects of the "real world" it may point to. So Cubism leads to abstraction.

And so for Gertrude Stein writing began with paintings. She says she learned from Cezanne, at first, what could be done with words. Each part of the painting was essential, each gesture, each mark: "It was not solely the realism of the characters but the realism of the composition which was the important thing . . . " It would not be necessary to make the fruit appear ripe and edible. The fruit was no more essential to the composition than the leg of the table, or the curve of the cloth, or that dark vertical line that does not seem to be a part of any window or chair or table.

"In writing about painting," she says in "What Are Master-pieces," "I said that a picture exists for and in itself and the painter has to use objects, landscapes, and people as a way the only way that he is able to get the picture to exist." Similarly, couldn't literature use objects, landscapes, and people to talk itself into existence? Then the composition of the surface might make its own, separate demands. In her 1923 essay "Cezanne," she wrote:

> Bees in a garden make a specialty of honey and so does honey. Honey and prayer. Honey and there. There where the grass can grow nearly four times yearly.

And how it moves along might become what it has to say. The name could be the sign of itself alone. The sentence could be like the stroke of the brush. "I came to the conclusion," she says in the second of her four Chicago lectures, "that poetry was a calling an intensive calling upon the name of anything."

A picture by Cézanne will appear now as a bowl of apples, now as a woman, now as a distant blue mountain. Moving closer, woman, fruit, and mountain disappear, giving way to the appearance of the strokes of the brush—things in themselves. Perhaps paint is what we were looking at all the time. And yet: "I felt that the thing I got from Cézanne," Stein told Haas, "was not the last composition."

"When a form is realized," Picasso had said, "it is there to live its own life." But words for Gertrude Stein had not yet come into their own life, or (as she claimed) they had lost their way sometime around the end of the nineteenth century. So Stein felt it her task to recapture "the value of the individual word." If this is no small task, Stein was not hampered by lack of ambition. Indeed, one of the central aims of the *Autobiography* is to display Gertrude Stein as a genius.

■

Toward the end of the *Autobiography*, Stein's more difficult work is described as "the destruction of associational emotion in poetry and prose." Her small book from 1914, *Tender Buttons,* embodies this aim. It begins with three sentences entitled "A Carafe, that Is A Blind Glass":

A kind in glass and a cousin, a spectacle and nothing strange a single hurt color and an arrangement in a system to pointing. All this and not ordinary, not unordered in not resembling. The difference is spreading.

The pieces in this book form "an arrangement in a system to pointing," but the words do not gesture away from themselves. They point at themselves and at each other: words as things, as objects on the page, as individual presences ("hurt color," for example, or a blind glass). On the other hand, the phrase I've just excerpted from Stein's passage is the one that makes the most "sense," and I've used it in a way that presents it as an idea, not a thing. Does her work invite such a move? Sometimes it does, and sometimes it doesn't. From "Rooms," the last section of the book:

> The care with which the rain is wrong and the green is wrong and the white is wrong, the care with which there is a chair and plenty of breathing. The care with which there is incredible justice and likeness, all this makes a magnificent asparagus, and also a fountain.

So with care anything could be an asparagus, or a fountain, artichoke or salad dressing, apple, cup, table, elephant, a shawl which is a hat or a red balloon, which is a wedding or a chair, or incredible justice. Anything incredible could appear in the system of the sentence. But to write *about* Stein in this way is to start to sound like her, and to risk parodying her. "Cocoa and clear soup and oranges and oat-meal." Words tumble into each other, yielding up parts of their meaning, spreading into difference, then doubleness, then back again into what that individual word might be by itself.

> Sugar any sugar, anger every anger, lover sermon lover, centre no distractor, all order is in a measure.

Interestingly, three of the major writerly features of the pieces in *Tender Buttons* are alliteration, rhyme, and repetition, mainstays of poetry. Are these the fixed points around which the apparent chaos of those separate words attempt to dance? Indeed, much of Stein's difficult work inclines toward the condition of poetry, poetry that feels like a combination of Imagism and Surrealism combined with a strong element of philosophy: Philosophical Imagistic Surrealism, if you will. As poetry—if it is helpful to call it poetry—its genre may belong entirely to Gertrude Stein. But what if wordplay becomes *merely* wordplay, suggesting nothing beyond or behind it—no philosophical or literary ideas, no visible images, no sense of a subconscious or a dream-world, nothing half-perceived and alluring? Is this her final ambition? If so, one of the dangers is (as we know) that any word or phrase, repeated often enough, will certainly lose its meaning and in some way go dead, if only for a moment. From "An Acquaintance with Description" (1926):

> Let it be when it is mine to be sure let it be when it is mine when it is mine let it be to be sure when

it is mine to be sure let it be let it be let it be to be
sure let it be to be sure when it is mine to be sure

And so on, for many more lines. Could this be "the value of the individual word," or only a drone in a mind that has begun to lose hold of the word altogether? Could words be stripped of their associations by urging them toward the condition of song or chant? By fragmenting and twisting grammar? By ordering a sentence so that even articles and prepositions would seem to take on the color and value of nouns and verbs?

Finally it was impossible: the meaning, the associational emotion, could not be destroyed. It could be baffled but not annihilated. Unlike the paint that became apples and mountains, or within both simply shapes on the flat inflexible surface of the canvas, words clung to their meanings. And the mind of the listener also clung to meaning. She told Haas:

> I took individual words and thought about them until I got their shape and volume complete and put them next to another word and at the same time I found out very soon that there is no such thing as putting them together without sense. I made innumerable efforts to make words write without sense and found it impossible. Any human being putting down words had to make sense out of them.

Gertrude Stein's most difficult work is an adventure on the edge of language that was bound to fail—work that was destined to alienate those readers so charmed by the *Autobiography*, work that Janet Malcolm wickedly describes as treating the reader like "an uninvited guest arriving on the wrong night at a dark house." No one could destroy "associational emotion in poetry and prose." But Gertrude Stein is not always well served by the explanations, justifications, and extraordinary claims she makes for her own work. So it becomes difficult simply to look at and listen to what she has done. Here is one sentence from *A Long Gay Book* (written in 1913, but not published until 1933):

> Please the spoons, the ones that are silver and have sugar and do not make mischief later, do not ever say more than listening can explain.

Listening can explain: this seems to me like a more helpful key to her work, and to that particular sentence, than the grand idea of the destruction of associational emotion—but again that phrase *is* an idea, and a very sensible one, as opposed to the playful surreality of those potentially mischievous spoons.

In fact she does not destroy emotion, or sense, and indeed the sentences themselves do not really attempt such a destruction. Instead, sense and emotion, and images and meanings, are fragmented and displaced. When a sentence slides in and then out of what "seems" to make sense, such a gesture depends upon the possibility and the presence of something like "sense" to begin with. An image will appear, then disappear, then reappear and—like a magic trick—dismantle itself as the eye moves along the surface. But more

than what listening can explain can become less than
what listening might mean.

■

I'm not really sure what that previous sentence—my
sentence—really means. This essay, though significantly
revised, was originally written in the mid-1970s, and in
those days I valued opacity more than I do now. Now I am
more impatient, desiring, at best, clarity that gives way to a
kind of mystery that might in turn be described as a sort of
seeming opacity. This is quite different from confusion that
tries to get by on charm—or music—alone, just as playing
with sense is different from nonsense. In the last sentence
of the previous paragraph I feel I have been absorbed
into bad Stein-speak, the repetition that loops around, the
"statements" that appear to cancel each other out.

Whether I knew what my original sentence meant
when I wrote it, I can't remember. Perhaps I was so
enamored of Stein's twisty language that I was pleased
to sound like her by playing a variation upon her theme.
Quoting Gertrude Stein and writing (a little) like Stein,
are, in fact, two of the significant pleasures of reading her.
But to return to Stein herself: ". . . do not ever say more
than listening can explain."

That sentence fragment (even if the spoons are "responsible" for it, which the syntax leaves unclear) makes
a great deal of sense to me, and I take it to mean: Do not
say more than the attentive act of listening is capable of
intelligently grasping. In this regard, brevity is one of the
major values of *Tender Buttons*, at least of those pieces that

are brief. Doesn't she often say much more than listening can explain, or even tolerate? The rewards of very close attention start to flag when extended over too large a canvas, causing even a sympathetic reader to become irritated. But let's give Stein the benefit of our doubts. What can listening explain?

To think further about this, let's take a look at a longer passage from *Tender Buttons*. The following is part of the middle of the third piece in the book, which is entitled "A Substance in a Cushion":

> What is the use of a violent kind of delightfulness if there is no pleasure in not getting tired of it. The question does not come before there is a quotation. In any kind of place there is a top to covering and it is a pleasure at any rate there is some venturing in refusing to believe nonsense. It shows what use there is in a whole piece if one uses it and it is extreme and very likely the little things could be dearer but in any case there is a bargain and if there is the best thing to do is to take it away and wear it and then be reckless be reckless and resolved on returning gratitude.
>
> Light blue and the same red with purple makes a change. It shows that there is no mistake. Any pink shows that and very likely it is reasonable. Very likely there should not be a finer fancy present. Some increase means a calamity and this is the best preparation for three and more being together. A little calm is so ordinary and in any case there is sweetness and some of that.
>
> A seal and matches and a swan and ivy and a suit.

Perhaps there is a connection of some interesting sort between a seal and a suit that I've been too inattentive to grasp. Perhaps I'm looking for the wrong sort of clue, or trying to solve the wrong kind of mystery. Listening has explained almost nothing to me here, although Stein has made me aware of a kind of vibration between a lack of sense and nonsense—nonsense which, following her words, one might venture to find and then refuse to believe.

What I do find particularly alluring in this passage is the beginning: "What is the use of a violent kind of delightfulness if there is no pleasure in not getting tired of it." This statement feels like a gloss on the work itself. Insofar as *Tender Buttons* produces "a violent kind of delightfulness" (and it often does), then our response is without pleasure if we cannot, at some point, get tired of it. ("It" here could mean either the work or our response to it, or both.) This might be an argument for brevity. And I like reading her sentence that way. But the double negative makes the sentence difficult to unravel. It seems like it could mean the opposite of what I want it to mean. That is, there is no use in a "violent kind of delightfulness" if there is pleasure in getting tired of it. I'm not at all sure if I have read Stein's sentence correctly either way. And a further complication arises from the fact that her sentence, though lacking a question mark, is a question, one that I've turned into a statement. "What is the use . . . " What is the answer? What, exactly, was the question?

Nevertheless, I feel there is both pleasure and value in *trying* to read Stein's sentence, and I might suggest that this attempt is more exciting—even more rewarding—

than getting the meaning "right." After all, she could have said what she meant. This is what still draws me to Stein. The linking of matches and ivy does little for me. But the conjunction of violence and delightfulness is wonderfully provocative. And provocation, I believe, is finally her most singular achievement.

■

I want to trust that literature, especially radical literature, instructs us, as we read it, about how it wants to be read. Similarly, radically new art shows us different ways of looking, as long as we are open to looking in a different way. As we know, what was once new will eventually— and sometimes very quickly—become conventional. So it is useful—and, yes, pleasurable—to value and even in- dulge our bafflement in the face of strangeness. As Jackson Pollock said of his drip paintings: "The strangeness will wear off . . ." What once was shocking all too quickly becomes wallpaper for a corporate boardroom.

In his essay "The Moment of Cubism," John Berger writes:

> The metaphorical model of Cubism is the *diagram*: the diagram being a visible, symbolic representation of invisible processes, forces, structures . . . The Cubists created the possibility of art revealing processes instead of static entities. The content of their art consists of various modes of interaction . . . Rather than ask of a Cubist picture: Is it true? or: Is it sincere? one should ask: Does it continue?
>
> Gertrude Stein's difficult art chronologically

surrounds the amiability of the *Autobiography*. But I want to suggest that the *Autobiography* can help us read what otherwise we might find annoyingly opaque. And Cubism helps as well. Stein's art also consists of various "modes of interaction": between different aspects of the same word; between apparent sense and obscurity; between silence and repetition, or stillness and movement; between the listener and the thing heard, misheard, or ignored. Rather than ask: What is it saying? or: Does it make sense? we might begin by asking: How does it move?

This returns us, perhaps by a circuitous route, to Stein's appreciation of detective fiction: "I never try to guess who has done the crime . . . but I like somebody being dead and how it moves along." I want to connect Berger's "Does it continue?" and Stein's "how it moves along." Since movement was one of the central problems of the construction of the *Autobiography*, how it moves along is useful to think about in approaching any of her work. The clarity of the *Autobiography* gives us access to the complications of *Tender Buttons*.

Quoting Berger again, we might call Stein's experimental work "a visible, symbolic representation of invisible processes," the elements of which both collide and snuggle up to each other.

> I myself have had no liking for violence and have always enjoyed the pleasure of needlework and gardening. I am fond of paintings, furniture, tapestry, houses and flowers and even vegetables

and fruit-trees. I like a view, but I like to sit with my back to it.

So Alice B. Toklas begins the *Autobiography*, in a tone not unlike a response to a tiresome questionnaire: Tell us a little about yourself—for example your likes and dislikes. Objects, landscapes, and people—these, at first, are what can be most easily seen. They are, like the apples in the painting by Cézanne, an invitation to move farther into the surface. Just as any object or landscape could be the subject of a painting, any remark could also be the material for the sentence that could become literature. It is only necessary to read a biography of Gertrude Stein in which one encounters the same stories and gossip to see that her book is concerned with more than the recitation of amusing anecdotes.

When she told Hemingway imperiously that remarks are not literature, perhaps she did not explain herself. Perhaps Hemingway simply ignored her, knowing by then what kinds of sentences he wished to write. Or perhaps Gertrude Stein understood that she would not take her own advice, and that the genius she so often insisted she was could transform mere remarks into a masterpiece. But she would let Alice say it for her: "And she has and this is it."

Ghosts and Their Discontents

What do ghosts want? Revenge is one traditional desire, or a proper burial, or the revelation of some important information (frequently involving hidden treasure, or the location of a body that needs to be properly buried); or, finally, nothing at all. In terms of revenge, *Hamlet* remains the greatest—and strangest—of ghost stories. The apparition of Hamlet's father appears twice to speak to his son. The first meeting, on the battlements of Elsinore, involves the disclosure of what Hamlet senses, or even wishes to believe: that his father has been murdered by his uncle, who has married his mother. At this point the ghost, who announces he will be "brief," is extremely long-winded. But it all comes down to: *Kill the king*. Note that the ghost can't do this by himself. His only power is to appear and to speak, not to act.

The ghost's second visitation is in Hamlet's mother's bedroom, and one striking fact of this scene is that Gertrude does not see the ghost, and therefore assumes (as others already have) that Hamlet has gone crazy. Seeing what's not there is a sure sign of madness. Yet *we* see what Gertrude does not: the actor we've consented to accept as a ghost. And, again traditionally, ghosts can appear selectively. Animals, for example—dogs especially—may sense the presence of ghosts first. Gertrude's inability to see her dead husband proves nothing and complicates everything.

"Restless" is a word often applied to ghosts. They're unable to "rest" in the sense of not dying completely, of "giving up the ghost." Yet they're also worrisomely and unpredictably active. They appear and disappear, transparent yet present, haunting us. And unlike Hamlet's father, rarely do they speak. But they need us to understand, so they can be released. Or perhaps they simply haven't entirely left the world. They linger: an embodiment of memory, even if their bodies are so frail we might more accurately say they resemble memory itself in its passing. They are what we will forget, or what we try to forget. Or else: *We* are what *they* are unable to forget.

"What is a ghost?" Stephen Dedalus asks "with tingling energy" in James Joyce's *Ulysses*. "One who has faded into impalpability," he answers, "through death, through absence, though change of manners." That "tingling energy" feels as if Stephen has just seen a ghost, and his list of definitions is fascinating, the cause of the ghost being death, absence, or "change of manners." The first maintains the supernatural, while the other two suggest the impermanence of the human, as if you could become a ghost not by dying but by being forgotten. But if ghosts have "faded into impalpability," they must, for the living, be occasionally visible, unless we want to believe we are constantly surrounded by ghosts who do not or cannot reveal themselves to us. Which seems reasonable. And which raises the question: Whose memory, or loss of memory, creates the ghost? What do we think we've seen in the shadows? What do we imagine we've seen? So *memory*, fallible as it is, becomes inextricably linked to *imagination*.

A poem by Randall Jarrell called "A Ghost, a Real Ghost," ends with these lines: "A ghost, a real ghost / Has no need to die: what is he except / A being without access to the universe / That he has not yet managed to forget?" Ghosts are appropriately hard to grasp and define, and it's equally difficult to know what sort of world they inhabit, if they are "really" there. Is it a world that posits an afterlife they have not yet gained access to? Or is it our world, in which some residue—some "tingling energy"—of the actual person briefly remains?

How "actual" is their presence? Believing or disbelieving is central to the ghost story. Ghosts exist in the shadows of the uncanny. But the uncanny by definition is all shadows; that is, all uncertainty. Here is my dictionary's definition: "having or seeming to have a supernatural or inexplicable basis." The key is in that first "or." Having a supernatural basis puts us in a world with rules and assumptions, or at least possible rules and assumptions. "Seeming to have" leaves us in undefined territory.

In Sigmund Freud's wonderful and wonderfully bizarre essay "The 'Uncanny,'" one possible definition given is this, and here Freud is talking about the uncanny in art: ". . . an uncanny effect is often and easily produced by effacing the distinction between imagination and reality, such as when something that we have hitherto regarded as imaginary appears before us in reality, or when a symbol takes over the full function and significance of the thing it symbolizes . . ." Say we don't believe in ghosts. Then a ghost appears before us in reality. Or have we imagined it? No, the dog knows it's there; then someone else sees it, too. How much do the rules of our world need to change to accommodate this appearance? We're uncertain, we hesitate. The uncanny exists in the space of that hesitation.

When we read a story we have to imagine. We also

have to wonder about the storyteller—not the author so much as the narrator. What sort of reality are we consenting to in this fiction, or being lured into believing? That seems appropriately to lead to what I consider (after *Hamlet*, perhaps), the greatest of all ghost stories, Henry James's *The Turn of the Screw*.

I started teaching in 1976, and I clearly remember my freshman-level classes on *The Turn of the Screw*. At the end of the first of two meetings, after some close reading of the ghosts' various appearances, I could ask, "But what if there are no ghosts?" And I could expect a palpable gasp. Now students are too smart (or perhaps the book has migrated to high school curricula). Now there's always someone waving his or her hand right at the beginning wanting to announce that there aren't ghosts, just a crazy governess, as if that settled it.

But the problem here is assuming that the "solution" lies in one direction *or* the other. Either we have a ghost story that reveals itself to be a psychological drama (thus changing various sets of rules), or a pure ghost story in which the governess's reading of the situation is correct and defines the rules. I want to suggest that the novel is designed to triumph over this apparent choice, and so keep us in a state of hesitation. Here's what James craftily says of the book in his preface to the New York edition:

> The merit of the tale, as it stands, is accordingly, I judge, that it has struggled successfully with its dangers . . . I need scarcely add after this that it is a piece of ingenuity pure and simple, of cold artistic calculation, an *amusette* to catch those

not easily caught (the "fun" of the capture of the merely witless being ever but small), the jaded, the disillusioned, the fastidious.

James's famously complicated sentences seem here designed to create more problems and clarify very little. But he's not just being wordy: he doesn't want to give things away. Who are those "not easily caught," who are apparently the opposite of the "merely witless," who are no fun to fool? They are "the jaded, the disillusioned, the fastidious." They are not the eager believers in ghosts, or they wouldn't be jaded. They are those who think they have the answers, the students waving their hands to reveal the secret of the crazy narrator; they are all of us who haven't read really carefully, but *think* we have.

Where does that leave us? Are there ghosts in *The Turn of the Screw* or not? If the answer is that if by the end we still don't know, then the book remains in the world of the uncanny. No governing rules have been revealed. So was it all just a trick—being fooled into believing one reading, then having that rug pulled out from under us?

Let's go back to the story's opening, which is a prologue, containing a story within another story. The first sentence begins: "The story had held us, round the fire, sufficiently breathless . . . " This is a different ghost story that we're never given, but it prefigures the one told "with quiet art" by a man named Douglas, whom the unnamed "I" (not James, or maybe James) calls "our friend." Douglas's story, the narrator says, requires "a few words of prologue"— that is, a prologue within James's prologue, spoken by Douglas, but conveyed to us by that "I." What Douglas then reads aloud is the unnamed governess's handwritten tale, which is the rest of the novel. But what we're reading is the "exact" transcription the unnamed speaker possesses—yet another step removed from the real thing. If all this seems confusing, it is, and no doubt is meant to be. How many layers of stories are there, how many occasions for what's "exact" to be corrupted?

The novel ends with the death of a child—Miles. The governess's final sentences are: "I caught him, yes, I held him—it may be imagined with what a passion; but at the end of a minute I began to feel what it truly was that I held. We were alone with the quiet day, and his little heart, dispossessed, had stopped."

Miles is "dispossessed," but has his soul been saved, or has he been killed by the governess's fierce possessiveness? Has he literally been *scared to death*? There's evidence in the book to support either view, but first we should ask this question: What's missing here? If a story begins with an elaborate prologue, don't we expect an epilogue where our questions would be answered, or at least articulated? We'd go back to Douglas and his audience, that little seminar of enthralled believers beside the fire, and they'd talk about what they have just heard, and we have just read. What James cleverly—and almost secretly—withholds from us is nothing less than the ending of his story.

It's worth reminding ourselves that James's initial readers would not have encountered his novel as a classic "text" with footnotes and a smart introduction. The story was published as a serial in *Collier's Weekly* in 1898 in twelve installments. If I'd been a reader then I'm sure I would have thought, 'Wait a minute, there must be more!

Where's installment number thirteen? Where's the explanation?' The book then becomes about our need for explanation, and the difficulties of interpretation, both of the governess's reading of her situation, and of our reading of her reading.

Here are some specific possibilities, beyond the obvious two, which are (1) there *are* ghosts, they're evil, the governess is right, and she saves Miles's soul, but kills him in the process. (2) There are no ghosts, and the governess is mad. The children are innocent, and the "evil" is in the governess, though she never realizes it (as least as far as our version of her story goes).

Now consider two more explanations: (3) There are ghosts, but only the governess can see them. The children don't see them (as they repeatedly insist), but the evil ghosts win by working through the weakness of the governess, that weakness being her willingness—or her need—to believe in ghosts. Or (4) There are ghosts, the governess is right, but the children may or may not see them. The ghosts *may or may not be malevolent*, although the governess, who is young, and whose reading seems to consist of gothic thrillers, *assumes* they must be. In both of my second two possibilities, the children—whether innocent or not—are overwhelmed by the governess's disastrous act of misreading.

Consider the various ghostly appearances. What do they consist of? Quint, the estate's handyman, stares. Miss Jessel, the previous governess, silently weeps. As ghosts they do nothing but look, bow their heads, linger, and fade away. They seem, if anything, not malevolent, but profoundly sad. Then where exactly is the *horror?* The governess provides it with her vivid language, and, at the end, her passionate exorcism. Peter Quint, the governess insists, is "the hideous *author* of all our woe" (emphasis mine). That's what she sees and no doubt believes. And we can see this with her, or we can pause and worry.

As metaphors, these ghosts are essentially unstable. They could represent sadness and loss, or, following the governess's lead, damnation and horror, or repressed sexuality that might lead to a different kind of damnation and horror. As ghosts, their sad and speechless presence—if indeed they are even there—is an emptiness that needs to be filled with the language of revulsion or fear or perhaps, on our part, sympathy. And this raises the question: If they *are* there, what do they want? A better question might be: What does James want by suggesting that they may or may not be there? What is the trap he has set for the jaded and the disillusioned?

One of the best answers to this question is a sentence from an essay written in 1920 by Harold C. Goddard, and titled "A Pre-Freudian Reading of *The Turn of the Screw*." Goddard says, "A man with an hypothesis runs the risk of finding confirmation for it everywhere."

And in the book, a woman with an active imagination —"young, untried, nervous," we're told in the prologue— sees what she wishes to see. And sometimes, significantly she doesn't even need to look to be sure. Early on in the story, the former governess, Miss Jessel, "appears," as the present governess sits with Miles's younger sister, Flora, beside a small lake:

Suddenly . . . I became aware that . . . we had an interested spectator. The way this knowledge gathered in me was the strangest thing in the world—the strangest, that is, except the very much stranger in which it quickly merged itself . . . I began to take in with certitude and yet without direct vision the presence, a good way off, of a third person . . . There was no ambiguity in anything; none whatever at least in the conviction I from one moment to another found myself forming as to what I should see straight before me and across the lake as a consequence of raising my eyes.

She doesn't raise her eyes until the end of that section of the story, and even then we're not told what she sees. But what do we imagine, dangerous as it is to imagine anything in James's tale, impossible as it is not to? Before she looks up the governess congratulates herself on her bravery: "Then . . . I faced what I had to face." But the most wonderful sentence in this section occurs at the end of the penultimate paragraph: "Nothing was more natural than that these things should be the other things they absolutely were not." So much for there being "no ambiguity in anything." Her language betrays her. Or reveals her. If there's a "secret" here it lies in the troubled syntax of the sentences Henry James has created for her.

Finally, we cannot resolve the problem of the existence of these ghosts, but the problem of our need to know can be confronted. Our desire is to be sure, to interpret "correctly," which is the governess's desire as well. Her quandary within the story becomes ours as readers. But we must save ourselves from her certainties. Just as there is no way to see without interpreting, there is no way to read without assumptions, prejudices, and hypotheses, as if those ghosts were emblems not of horror but of uncertainty.

Ghosts fade "into impalpability," as Stephen Dedalus says. Or they are in the process of disappearing, although sometimes their apparent refusal to separate themselves from life is what most troubles us. But why shouldn't they resist leaving the world we also wish to cling to? They are too much like us, and one sign of this is that they live in our houses. Or what once were their houses.

It is hard to separate ghosts from homes—the haunted house seems synonymous with the ghost. Ghosts lend themselves to the intimacy of the home, and the secret knowledge available to those who are mostly invisible. Metaphorically, the home becomes the body, as the ghost haunts both a literal and a psychological space. Emily Dickinson captures this duality beautifully:

> One need not be a Chamber—to be Haunted—
> One need not be a House—
> The Brain has Corridors—surpassing
> Material Place—
>
> Far safer, of a Midnight Meeting
> External Ghost
> Than its interior Confronting—
> That Cooler Host.

Far safer, through an Abbey gallop,
The Stones a'chase—
Than Unarmed, one's a'self encounter—
In lonesome Place—

Ourself behind ourself, concealed—
Should startle most—
Assassin hid in our Apartment
Be Horror's least.

The Body—borrows a Revolver—
He bolts the Door—
O'erlooking a superior spectre—
Or More—

Her metaphor for the mind is the house—those "Corridors" in the brain. And this surpasses, but does not cancel out, the actual "Chamber," though the most frightening ghost is interior and self-created: "That Cooler Host." In Dickinson's metaphor, the ghost has taken control of the house, has become its host, and so possessed—and dispossssed—the real owner, in terms of property and the space of the imagination.

Ghosts appear as what we were or will become. They confuse and call into question both seeing and believing, as if to dismantle the old adage that "Seeing is believing," or turn it into "Believing is seeing." Therefore believing hard enough conjures up the visible, provides the ocular "evidence" that solves the crimes, since the ghost story is often a detective story as well—uncovering and bringing to light the crimes of the past, or bringing back what should have remained hidden, or discovering for certain what was never there to begin with. This trembling tension—between truth and fiction, belief and disbelief, life and death—is the essence of the stories we read late at night and with pleasuire to frighten ourselves.

Although in this essay I provided no Jamesian prologue, let me end with an epilogue. And in the spirit of Henry James let me try to explain as little as possible.

In a very short story entitled "Unhappiness" by Franz Kafka, the narrator is visited by the ghost of a child. "Like a small ghost a child blew in from the pitch-dark corridor, where the lamp was not yet lit, and stood a-tiptoe on a floorboard that quivered imperceptibly." Note that the child is "like a small ghost," but she is a ghost.

They talk. "Are you really looking for me? Isn't there some mistake?" the narrator asks. "Hush, hush," says the child, "it's all right . . . Just be easy in your mind." They talk further, mostly about whether or not the door is shut. The narrator says, "I'm so pleased that you've come at last." The ghost-child says, "No stranger could come any nearer to you than I am already by nature. You know that, too, so why all this pathos?" The ghost's last line is, "I don't know anything." Then the speaker leaves his room and on the stairway encounters another tenant from his floor.

"I've just had a ghost in my room," the narrator says, and the tenant replies, "How true. But what if one doesn't believe in ghosts at all?" And the speaker says, "Well, do you think I believe in ghosts? But how can my not believing help me?"

"Quite simply," the other man replies. "You don't need to feel afraid if a ghost actually turns up." "Oh," the speaker answers, "that's only a secondary fear. The real fear is a fear of what caused the apparition. And that fear doesn't go away." Then the speaker adds, "Obviously you've never spoken to a ghost. One never gets straight information from them. It's just a hither and thither. These ghosts seem to be more dubious about their existence than we are, and no wonder, considering how frail they are."

Perhaps we should just admire the beautiful strangeness of these two encounters. How matter-of-fact they are, and how unsettling. And yet: "Hush," the child says, "it's all right. Just be easy in your mind."

But it's not all right. The real fear is the fear of what causes the apparition, and that's hidden in our minds: "Ourself behind ourself, concealed." How afraid should we be of what's out there in the dark? How afraid should we be of ourselves, and what we *think* we've seen?

Poetry and Dreams

> *Poems are like dreams; in them you put what you don't know you know.*
> —Adrienne Rich

My two best friends and I were touring France. We were staying at a place called *The Hotel of 100 Strangers*, but soon I wandered off and became lost, sometimes moving between room and room or house and house, and once finding myself near an old forest at dusk that bordered lawns that looked vaguely like a golf course. Finally I was in another hotel and asked how far it was to *The Hotel of 100 Strangers*, and the deskman told me, Oh, it was very far. I was appalled at the distance he pointed out on a map, as he told me it was at least a six-hour walk. I couldn't believe I'd been walking already for six hours. Then he said rather wistfully, "It's a shame we're not doing 'The Reading of the Bones' today, because there would be a lot more people here." Presumably someone from this group would have been willing to take me back to *The Hotel of 100 Strangers*. But it wasn't the day for "The Reading of the Bones," though as I looked over his shoulder I could see, dimly, tall glass cabinets full of very large bones, like the tusks of animals.

■

Dreams are the sleeping imagination's narrative of transformations. Poems are the waking imagination's narrative of change. In this regard, I'd want to identify "transformation" as a process that is mysterious and disjunctive, and "change" as an alternate process that is conscious and connective. Then we might say that a poem that uses dreams or dream-like material is a record of the way the imagination moves from one to the other.

■

And yet, don't dreams feel perfectly sensible when we're experiencing them? The quick, cinematic cut from one scene to another isn't met with incredulity by the dreamer —it's just what happens: suddenly you are somewhere else. This seems natural, even if, upon reflection and re-membrance, it only seems that way. Yet its strangeness may also appear connected to some central concern, perhaps now lost, or partially recovered, like memory itself, or the revisions of memory.

■

Consider the following entry from Nathaniel Haw-thorne's *American Notebook*: "To write a dream, which shall resemble the real course of a dream, with all its inconsistency, its eccentricities and aimlessness—with nevertheless a leading idea running through the whole." That is the problem for the artist who attempts to use dream material. Is it possible to represent convincing-ly the anxieties, disturbances, fascinations, and genuine mysteries of a dream (that is, the "real course" of it) while at the same time planting a "leading idea" running all the way through? Hawthorne wants both the shape of the idea and the appearance of the fragmentary and even apparently random qualities of the dream. But if the idea controls a poem or story too much, the authenticity of the dream material is diminished, and turned into mere emblem and symbol, calculated and without mystery.

■

"Do not try to be faithful," Stephen Dunn's poem "How to Write a Dream Poem" begins. "Change the tunnel to a mountain road / in a South American country, Bolivia / if you need those sounds, / otherwise Chile is a place where / something unfortunate might happen / to someone like you." This poem, Dunn writes, is "a series of assertions that were tantamount to saying: be a fictionist. From then on I tried to invent and simultaneously parody as many dream clichés as I could." Two-thirds of the way through this faux dream, Dunn becomes more reflective: "In dreams shape-shifting is as normal / as fabulous acts of revenge. But everything in your poem / should depend on arrangement / more than statement, on enchantment / more than any specific, disabling fear."

So Hawthorne's "leading idea" must involve both content *and* structure. Probably the structure precedes the idea. Structure allows content to make itself visible.

■

The tactic of moving in a dream-like way is a kind of surrealism, and need not be identified as representing the actuality of dreaming. For example, "The Infirmament," a poem by the contemporary American surrealist

Dean Young, contains the following lines about halfway through:

> A father may say nothing to a son for years.
> A wife may keep something small folded deep
> in her underwear drawer. Clouds come in
> resembling the terrible things we believe
> about ourselves, a rock comes loose
> from a ledge, the baby just cries
> and cries. Doll in a chair,
> windshield wipers, staring off
> into the city lights.

The first four and a half lines here seem to connect to each other, though neither the father nor the wife appears elsewhere in the poem. The connective tissue involves silence and deception leading to those "terrible things we believe /about ourselves." But the rock and the baby don't quite seem to fit, even though *their* sentences are linked by comma splices to the earlier material. After that the poem moves in an even more disjunctive way, linking through sentence fragments the doll, the windshield wipers, and the city lights. The connective relationships here are all but invisible, though the syntactical structure does join them, enabling the poem to manage the maximum amount of mysterious dream-like material without everything flying apart.

The surrealist image, Young writes in *The Art of Recklessness*, "seeks to create and transmit by simultaneously hazarding disconnection and asserting reconnection, disconnecting a thing from its stagnated context, then providing another thing equally disenfranchised from the ordinary so that a spark can occur between them . . . "

■

Although dreams themselves may seem curiously coherent to the dreamer, a dream poem that merely offers itself the freedom to move anywhere without any coherent structure to contain it is doomed to annoying insignificance. There are no sparks, because no aesthetic choices have been made. Turning again to Young: "Clarity results from the intensity of choice. Meaninglessness results not from too little but too much meaning. A string of randomly selected words is a site of nearly unlimited interpretations generating only vagaries because no decision has been made."

■

It's hard to identify in the work of others a poem designed to present an actual dream without admitting it to be a dream. Let me risk embarrassment, then, by choosing one of my own failed poems. Many years ago I had a dream that I found haunting and disturbing and interesting. I told it to others who felt, or said they felt, similarly. So I tried to import it directly into a poem, where it just sat there, all of its mysterious impact gone. The images, I later realized, were insufficiently surprising *for a poem*, but most of all, the poem lacked a structure—or a way of thinking—to contain and consider those images. This kind of poem, in Dunn's terms, is trying to be too faithful.

It has not yet found a way to become a poem. My dream poem began:

> Already
> I have entered the house.
> You are there waiting, and we appear
> together in an immense attic,
> darkness falling away beneath us,
> deeper than I can think.
>
> Near me, through the middle
> of a heavy wooden beam, one bright spike
> impales, skinned and bleeding,
> a tiny hand like a child's hand.
>
> *Look!* The fingers begin to move.
>
> *Come up to the roof,* you reply.
>
> We discover a huge bird
> attacking a rabbit.

And so on. The dream occurred many years ago, back in the mid-1970s. When it became apparent to me that the poem was relying on the dream rather than using it, I tried admitting this within the poem:

> I know
> the dream's mine.
> One more troublesome problem—
> what could I expect it to say

to you, to anyone,
or now, to me.

This, obviously, is less an engaging turn than a kind of throwing up of my hands. Everything that was powerful about the dream itself was first undercut by the attempt to turn it into a poem, and then further diminished by the attempt to admit that turning it into a poem might be, in some way, the point. What point that could have been I do not know. And so the dream's insinuating incoherence became merely a series of discrete grotesque effects.

■

Since there is a kind of surreality to my poem, it seems important to distinguish between actual dreams and what we might call "the surreal," thinking of surrealism as that which opposes or abandons the logic of what we accept as the "real." And the reason for this, as least in surrealism's original French incarnation, was (as my dictionary says), to "express the workings of the subconscious by fantastic imagery and incongruous juxtaposition of subject matter." But actual dreams, I have asserted, aspire to the coherence of narrative, or assume it as a kind of camouflage. They are not experienced by the dreamer as surreal, even though they may seem so in retrospect. They are experienced as stories. And only in the fleeting moment before waking does the sleeper think, "Wait, that doesn't make sense."

The surreal, on the other hand, is designed to fend off sense, or to provoke us toward a different kind of sense. But when Young's "spark" does not occur, the poem slips into disconnection and incoherence.

As Wallace Stevens says, "The essential fault of surrealism is that it invents without discovering. To make a clam play an accordion is to invent, not to discover." True strangeness in art is difficult to achieve, because it must escape the merely symbolic or the merely allegorical just as it must escape the silliness of those clams. To invent without discovering isn't the "fault" of surrealism so much as it is its *danger*, its trap. Surrealism can be effective as long as its inventions are also discoveries.

■

Adrienne Rich's observation that poems are like dreams because "in them you put what you don't know you know," tells us as much about the making of art as it does about the condition of dreams. I think she means to offer the poet the privileges of the dreamer—that is, the discovery of connections not planned in advance. This separates the dreamer into dreamer and interpreter. The latter follows the former, or would seem to; though how much interpretation goes on *inside* a dream is certainly impossible to say. Moreover, the interpretation of the dream may be more or less sensible—and more or less revelatory—than the dream itself. Or we can imagine that the dream fades from memory and only the interpretation survives, disguised as a poem in which the writer can no longer distinguish what was actually dreamt from what was composed for the sake of the poem.

■

I've spoken of poems that move in a dream-like way (as in Dean Young) and poems that pretend to be dreams (my poem in its earliest version). A third category may be that of poems that utilize dreams and admit to doing so, making dreaming part of the dramatic situation. A good example of this is Anthony Hecht's wonderfully disturbing poem, "A Hill." And what is precisely disturbing about the poem is the negotiation—or the slippage—between dream and reality. The poem begins:

> In Italy, where this sort of thing can occur,
> I had a vision once—though you understand
> It was nothing at all like Dante's, or the visions of
>   saints,
> And perhaps not a vision at all.

Nowhere in the poem does Hecht use the word "dream"; it's always "vision," which (echoing Keats) is a kind of "waking dream," or a "day-dream," but with the implication of much more gravity and import. Yet Hecht begins his poem by disavowing the weightiness of "vision," declaring that his was nothing like Dante's, nothing like the visions of saints, and perhaps not worthy of the grand term "vision" at all. This strategy of lowering expectations, nevertheless (as Hecht well knows) serves to invoke those saints and prophets and oracles whose visions were the revelations of a god, either in apparent reality or through the medium of the dream. The declaration that the poet's experience in Italy was perhaps "not a vision at all" serves him well; by avoiding the easily symbolic he creates a landscape (or two landscapes) both ambiguous and personal. Here is Hecht's poem in its entirety.

A Hill

In Italy, where this sort of thing can occur,
I had a vision once—though you understand
It was nothing at all like Dante's, or the visions of
    saints,
And perhaps not a vision at all. I was with some
    friends,
Picking my way through a warm sunlit piazza
In the early morning. A clear fretwork of shadows
From huge umbrellas littered the pavement and
    made
A sort of lucent shallows in which was moored
A small navy of carts. Books, coins, old maps,
Cheap landscapes and ugly religious prints
Were all on sale. The colors and noise
Like the flying hands were gestures of exultation,
So that even the bargaining
Rose to the ear like a voluble godliness.
And then, where it happened, the noises suddenly
    stopped,
And it got darker; pushcarts and people dissolved
And even the great Farnese Palace itself
Was gone, for all its marble; in its place
Was a hill, mole-colored and bare. It was very cold,
Close to freezing, with a promise of snow.
The trees were like old ironwork gathered for scrap

Outside a factory wall. There was no wind,
And the only sound for a while was the little click
Of ice as it broke in the mud under my feet.
I saw a piece of ribbon snagged on a hedge,
But no other sign of life. And then I heard
What seemed the crack of a rifle. A hunter, I
    guessed;
At least I was not alone. But just after that
Came the soft and papery crash
Of a great branch somewhere unseen falling to
    earth.

And that was all, except for the cold and silence
That promised to last forever, like the hill.

Then prices came through, and fingers, and I was
    restored
To the sunlight and my friends. But for more than
    a week
I was scared by the plain bitterness of what I had
    seen.
All this happened about ten years ago,
And it hasn't troubled me since, but at last, today,
I remembered that hill; it lies just to the left
Of the road north of Poughkeepsie; and as a boy
I stood before it for hours in wintertime.

The vision is, surprisingly, not of the great Farnese
Palace, or those "lucent shallows" out of which "a small
navy" is metaphorically imagined. Indeed, both the
warmth and extravagance of Italy and the lucidity of

Hecht's images lead unexpectedly to the bleakest of places (and of language): "a hill, mole-colored and bare. It was very cold, / Close to freezing, with a promise of snow." Then three events occur: he notices "a piece of ribbon snagged on a hedge," after which he hears what might be "the crack of a rifle," followed by the crash of "a great branch somewhere" out of sight.

How do these connect, if they do connect? The poet doesn't say. That was all, he declares, except "for the cold and silence / That promised to last forever, like the hill." His only interpretation of the vision is that it expresses "plain bitterness," which feels like much more than the bitterness of the weather.

Then we move ten years into the present moment when a second vision is offered to the poet: the hill itself, "just to the left / Of the road north of Poughkeepsie . . . " And this vision—or waking dream—is even more ambiguous than the "plain bitterness" of what he experienced in Italy. Here, just north of Poughkeepsie, he used to stand before that hill as a boy "for hours in wintertime." The surprise of this moment is *for hours*, and how much and how little it reveals. The hill once held a fascination for him. He stood *before it* as one might stand before a deity or an idol. And yet the uncanny power of the hill remains unexplained. Think of how much we're not told in this seemingly anecdotal poem: why he stood there as a boy; what the hill "meant" to him and why it demanded his attention; why it took him ten years to connect the Italian vision to an ordinary road in New York state; why the streets of Italy produced the vision in the first place; what the *vision* as opposed to a remembrance or a dream might demand of him; and finally how those three details and the judgment of "plain bitterness" which scared him for more than a week connect to the actual hill.

Through its strategy of withholding explanation, the poem feels like a true dream, full of an ominous but ambiguous sense of meaning in which, as in a fairy tale, we are given three clues that the speaker of the poem does not comment on—the rifle shot, the falling branch, and that "piece of ribbon snagged on a hedge." I don't know exactly what to do with the rifle shot and the branch, except to say that they both suggest violence, and that the second perception may cancel out the first—the crack was the branch breaking; there was no hunter; the speaker was alone. Or they were two separate occurrences. Or perhaps the sound of the branch falling is the result of something being shot. All might be true. But I find it hard not to think of that piece of ribbon as belonging to Faith in Nathaniel Hawthorne's story "Young Goodman Brown": "But something fluttered lightly down through the air and caught on the branch of a tree. The young man seized it, and beheld a pink ribbon."

In Hawthorne's story the truth is baffled by the possible reality of the dream, and so guilt appears in the guise of innocence, leaving Goodman Brown at the end bitter in ways no one can understand. Undeceived but self-deceived, "his dying hour was gloom." Has the witch's gathering truly been a satanic occasion, or a terrifying vision, or "merely" a dream? The story's narrator asks the same question: "Had Goodman Brown fallen asleep in the forest and only dreamed a wild dream of a witch-meeting? Be it so if you will." That final sentence is a startling move that turns everything over to the reader: make of it what you want, the story will clarify nothing. Was this all an invention, or was it the truth, or was it an invention that became the truth? Faith's ribbon is the emblem of this uncertainty.

■

A poem, as we know, can be a way of ordering memory, and revising, and even inventing it. In her novel *The Sleeping Beauty*, Elizabeth Taylor writes (not of Hawthorne's Goodman Brown, even if it could have been): "In dreams he had often before discovered the truth, or invented a condition which later became the truth." We should only add: Or invented a condition which he *took* to be the truth. Memory, after all, is itself a process of revision, although we may feel it's how we reclaim what actually happened. And then, in dreams, memory returns disguised as images that feel to us both mysterious and significant, the way they sometimes feel in poems.

■

As I have said, in the initial stages of composition, the poet may usefully claim some of the privileges of the dreamer. Any appearance may seem to precede the reason for its existence. Images need not immediately justify themselves. The surreal and the extravagant can look like their own rewards. But part of the allure of dreams—and of poems— resides in the possibility of interpretation, the uncovering of hidden significance. Similarly, to be interesting, what happens in a poem must appear at least *potentially* revelatory,

as in Hecht: "I saw a piece of ribbon snagged on a hedge
. . ."

As readers, we can enjoy what we don't at first fully
understand if we trust we're being led somewhere. The
poem's *design* (or arrangement) will appear, and all of its
disparate moments will prove to be related and necessary.
And for the writer the process is the same: the writer tries
to establish those connections and make them work. "A
thing in a dream," Freud writes, "means what it recalls to
the mind." And a thing in a poem means what it has been
designed to recall to the reader's mind. Both dream and
poem are completed by acts of sympathetic understanding.

■

Now the reader may wish to recall my opening section
concerning that trip to France and those confusions at
The Hotel of 100 Strangers. As was probably apparent, this is
the transcription of an actual dream. Its accuracy can't be
known, of course. It is what it is: language as dream. Or:
language pretending to be a dream, the sleeping imagination's narrative of transformations. (And the dream,
as I recall it, was consistently insistent upon its narrative
coherence even when it appeared least coherent.) What
struck me most upon waking is probably obvious: the
wonderful name of the hotel, which sounds like it should
belong (and maybe does belong) in a poem by Charles
Simic. And secondly, "The Reading of the Bones." I like
the way the bones themselves are only briefly glimpsed,
and that the reading doesn't take place because I have
arrived on the wrong day. But of course I wasn't look-

ing for—and had never heard of—"The Reading of the Bones." I was trying to find my way back to my friends, back to *The Hotel of 100 Strangers*, where I assumed my friends still were.

Those seem to be the two most intriguing and essential elements of the dream. But a third has always stayed with me, which is that in my wanderings in the French landscape I came upon a dark woods bordered by what seemed to be a golf course. There were, of course, no golfers. But it looked like they could have been there, or once were.

■

In the summer of 2014, while I was working at The MacDowell Colony, I asked a fellow writer at breakfast for something to get me started that morning. She said, "Here's a Swahili proverb you can use: 'Who can understand women or the sky?'" Later she claimed I'd gotten it wrong, that the proverb was, "Who can understand women *and* the sky."

That's where I started, but as you will see in the poem that concludes this essay, I returned to my dream as I remembered it. I "mistook" the name of the hotel, writing "The Hotel of 1000 Strangers," but later, in some mistaken fidelity to the dream, I wanted to change 1000 back to 100, and was told by someone I trusted to leave it as it was—1000 sounded, or looked, more interesting than 100. The more strangers the better. Also, I had remembered quite clearly that the dream was set in France, but was convinced, for reasons that should be evident, given my introduction of Dante, to move the location to Italy. And my two friends became a single friend, for no reason I can recall.

I did not set out to reproduce the dream, which I had felt was interesting enough to write down (but which I did not consult until after I had finished the poem). When I'd tried to turn an "actual" dream into an actual poem, it was—as described earlier—a failure, because the poem merely attempted to replicate the dream. It took no imaginative risks of its own, and therefore established no Hawthornian "idea" running through it, no controlling shape that hadn't already existed. At the same time it was drained of its strangeness, since strangeness is a common currency in poetry.

■

What I like about the relationship of the poem "Women and the Sky" and my original "Hotel of 100 Strangers" dream is that I did not feel bound by the dream materials. I got to pick and choose. Yes, I'm sorry that I didn't get "The Reading of the Bones" in there, but it would have been too ominous, too obviously "significant." My imagination didn't need "The Reading of the Bones" so it didn't recover that phrase. Imagination changed 100 to 1000 for, let's say, sonic reasons. Imagination allowed that strange golf course to border the dark woods that would summon up Dante.

I suppose I could have invented all of this without the dream. And I don't have any idea how the Swahili proverb summoned up the dream material. If I told you

that I never actually had the dream I presented at the
beginning of this essay, and that all of the details in it were
made up one morning in New Hampshire for the sake of
the poem, I hope you would not feel tricked. I hope you
would think: "What difference does it make? One way or
the other, I don't need to know that."

Be it so if you will.

Women and the Sky

We were in Italy, my friend and I,
staying at *The Hotel of 1000 Strangers*,
when I got lost and wandered onto a golf course
bounded by a dark forest Dante would have
recognized. Back at the hotel someone

obviously famous was giving a lecture
about Swahili proverbs. "Who can understand
women or the sky?" he said, and paused
as if he wanted an answer. "Could that
involve two different people," I asked,

"one for the women and the other
for the sky?" "No," he replied, "and now
I would like to hear from someone else,
someone who has paid for this class."
Then I was lost again. I went into

a different hotel where some kind of party
was going on involving slabs of meat.
I asked the deskman, "Can you please

direct me to *The Hotel of 1000 Strangers*?"
"That hotel," he replied, "is much too far away."

"But I just came from there." "Well,"
he answered, "as the proverb says,
'A man who travels beyond time must enter
the dark woods where the dead still live.'"
"I don't want to do that," I told him.

"Alas, my friend, you have no choice."
Outside, a man who looked like Dante
from my old edition of the *Inferno*
asked me if I was ready. "Can you," I said,
"direct me to *The Hotel of 1000 Strangers*,

where even now my friend is waiting?"
"Are you in the middle of your life?"
Dante asked, and I said I was,
and he said, "Then it's the dark woods,"
and took hold of the edge of the cloak I seemed

to be wearing. "All right," I said, "but first
tell me who can understand women or the sky."
He paused. "Is that women *or* the sky or women
and the sky?" "Well," I answered, "I think the *and*
is implied in the *or*, as in 'What one person

can understand both women and the sky?'"
"It's ambiguous," Dante replied, and I had to agree.
We started walking. "A man and the sky
are two," he told me. "A man, a woman,
and the sky are also two. That's part

of the answer. But now you must try
to understand what the dead understand."
"Why do I have to know that?" I asked.
We entered the woods. Darkness descended.
"Listen," he said. "It's time to stop fooling around."

Acknowledgments

Grateful acknowledgment is made to the following publications in which these essays first appeared, in some cases in earlier versions.

First Loves, edited by Camela Ciuraru (Scribner, 2000): "First Love: On Lewis Carroll's 'Jabberwocky.'"

The Michigan Quarterly: "Remarks as Literature: *The Autobiography of Alice B. Toklas* by Gertrude Stein."

The New Ohio Review: "Thinking Out Loud: On Wisława Szymborska"; "Should Poems Tell the Truth?"; "In a Different Hour: Collaboration, Revision, and Friendship" (as "Where the Path Leads"). This essay also appeared in *The Room and the World: Essays on the Poet Stephen Dunn,* edited by Laura McCullough (Syracuse, 2014).

Plume: "Poetry and Stupidity." This essay was also featured on the website *Poetry Daily.*

Touchstones: American Poets on a Favorite Poem, edited by Robert Pack and Jay Parini (University Press of New England, 1995): "Why Don't We Say What We Mean? Robert Frost's 'Mending Wall.'"

The Writer's Chronicle: "Choosing the Wrong Subject" and "Poetry and Consolation."

My thanks to The MacDowell Colony where several of these essays were begun. And many thanks to Jim Schley at Tupelo Press for his scrupulous attention to this book.

Other Books from Tupelo Press

See our complete list at www.tupelopress.org